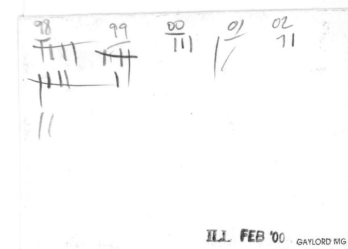

Medieval Britain

Medieval Britain

The Age of Chivalry

Lloyd and Jennifer Laing

Herbert Press

First published in Great Britain in 1996 by Herbert Press,
a division of A&C Black (Publishers) Limited,
35 Bedford Row, London WCIR 4JH

House editor: Nicky Shearman
Designed by Pauline Harrison

Set in Centaur
Typeset by Nene Phototypesetters, Northampton
Printed and bound in Hong Kong by South China Printing Co. (1988) Ltd

A CIP catalogue record for this book is available from the British Library

ISBN 1-871569-84-2

FRONTISPIECE: The Wriothesley Tomb, Titchfield Church, Hants (Philip Dixon)

The plan of Beaumaris Castle on page 53 is adapted from English Castles by
R. Allen Brown, Batsford 1977

Contents

Chronological Table

Royal Houses

Normans

William I (1066–1087)
1066 Battle of Hastings
1087 Domesday Book compiled

William II, Rufus (1087–1100)

Henry I (1100–1135)
1106 Conquest of Normandy

Stephen (1135–54) The Anarchy

Angevins & Plantagenets

Henry II (1154–89)
1170 Murder of Archbishop Thomas Becket

Richard I, The Lionheart (1189–99)

John (1199–1216)
1215 Magna Carta signed

Henry III (1216–72)
1258 Provisions of Oxford
1264 Barons' War. Simon de Montfort's parliament

Edward I (1272–1307)
1295 'Model Parliament'
1277–95 Campaigns in Wales
1295 Start of Scottish Wars of Independence

Edward II (1307–27)
1314 Scottish victory at Battle of Bannockburn

Edward III (1327–77)
1337 Beginning of Hundred Years' War with France
1348–9 Black Death
1346 Battle of Crécy, English victorious over French
1360 Treaty of Bretigny, England acquired Calais, and extensive territories in France

Richard II (1377–99)
1381 Peasants' Revolt

House of Lancaster

Henry IV (1399–1413)

Henry V (1413–22)

Henry VI (1422–61)
1444 Truce with France (end of Hundred Years War)
1455 Wars of the Roses begin
Second reign (1470–1)

House of York

Edward IV (1461–70)
Second reign (1471–83)

Edward V (1483)

Richard III (1483–5)
1485 Battle of Bosworth, Henry VII succeeds

Rulers of Scotland

David I (1124–1153)

Malcolm IV (1153–1165)

William the Lion (1165–1214)

Alexander II (1214–1249)

Alexander III (1249–1286)

Margaret (1286–1290)

John Baliol (1292–1296)

Robert Bruce (1306–1329)

David II (1329–1371)

Robert II (1371–1390)

Robert III (1390–1406)

James I (1406–1437)

James II (1437–1460)

James III (1460–1488)

James IV (1488–1513)

Preface

THE MEDIEVAL PERIOD saw the formation of the political and social structure of later Europe. It witnessed the first agrarian and industrial revolutions, saw the emergence of the town as a major economic and social force, and gave rise to the economic principles of capitalism that govern the twentieth century. It helped to establish such tenets as the work ethic, and the stranglehold on land ownership established by the Normans has had social and legal repercussions in Britain to the present day.

The Middle Ages produced architecture of unparalleled grandeur and aesthetic beauty as well as works of art and literature which still appeal. It dabbled in science as well as superstition, forged trading links which enabled the Tudor period to surge on to economic heights, reinforced and then began to break up a distinctive social system (feudalism), produced paupers and princes, knights, ladies and merchants. Because the vast majority of the population was tied to the land, with no powers and few rights, the upper elements in society were able to conduct their lives on a larger-than-life scale, and some manifestations of this, such as the great cathedrals, are fitting memorials.

It was the age of contrasts: of the Black Death, and also of chivalry, and a time when women could be regarded both as objects of veneration and as worthless chattels. It was a time when the abject poverty and slavery of the very poorest contrasted with the almost unlimited personal power and wealth of the richest: when some people were legally tied for life to the village in which they were born, while others travelled to the Holy Land in order to recapture Jerusalem from the Muslims.

There were advances in science and medicine which were happily juxtaposed with outrageously subjective superstitions and beliefs. There were many lighthearted amusements and pastimes during a period in which warfare was more prevalent than peace, and disease could wipe out whole communities within a week.

The struggles between king and barons eventually laid the foundations for the modern parliamentary system. The role of the Church was always vital, as is manifested in the fact that the most ouststanding works of art and architecture were produced to the glory of the Christian god.

This book considers mostly the existing material evidence in England, Wales and Scotland for the medieval period, from castles, cathedrals and houses to minor artworks, trade, the rise of towns and life in the countryside. A very brief historical framework is provided in the introduction. It is not an academic book — its aim is to introduce the lay person to the fascinations of the medieval period.

Introduction
The Medieval World

OPPOSITE: *Gloucester Cathedral, the choir (Edwin Smith, first published in* English Cathedrals *by Edwin Smith and Olive Cook, Herbert Press 1989)*

THE MIDDLE AGES traditionally begin with the arrival of William of Normandy in 1066, and end in 1485 with the Battle of Bosworth.

The Normans were in origin Vikings, who had settled in Normandy, married local women and adopted and developed a 'French' culture. Their expansion was rapid and Britain was seriously and lastingly affected when a complex succession dispute led William to defend his claim to the English throne. At Hastings he defeated and killed the English King Harold, establishing himself as monarch.

Resistance remained strong, particularly in the East and North. Between about 1068 and 1071 the north of England was devastated in what Simeon of Durham termed the 'Harrying of the North', when the region rebelled against the Norman overlords with disastrous and long-lasting effects. One Norman earl was killed, and thousands of English rallied against William. The problem was exacerbated for William as a fleet of 200 Danish ships entered the Humber and lent support to the rebels. York was sacked, and Norman control was lost. Although there had been an earlier rebellion (in Kent), William had dealt with it fairly mercifully. This time he took his army through Yorkshire, devastating the countryside. According to Orderic Vitalis, more than 100,000 people died of starvation in the aftermath, and Simeon of Durham's account describes the rotting bodies lining the roads of the region, and the plague which compounded northern misery.

Even this extent of devastation did not totally quell resistance. In 1071 an uprising in the Fens, led by the (later) legendary Hereward the Wake, was crushed due to monks from Ely revealing a secret route to the rebels' hideout. Even in comparatively peaceable Cheshire, by 1070 no fewer than 162 out of 264 estates were wholly or partially laid waste. It was not until the time of Edward I (1272–1307) that Wales, Scotland and Ireland came under Norman rule.

The imperialist Victorians saw the Normans as introducing superior culture to a backward nation. Reaction to this view in the post-World War II era tended to paint the Normans as primitive villains who trod mercilessly across the civilized face of Anglo-Saxon England. Opinion has now settled to a mid-way viewpoint, which sees the period as a comparatively brief interlude in which Norman inno-

9

William I silver penny, 'PAXS' type, Exeter mint (Lloyd Laing)

vations acted as a catalyst to speed up processes already at work in English society.

The Norman Conquest was a take-over at the top: the Anglo-Saxon world conquered by the Normans, in 1066, had a social pyramid headed by kings and high kings and with unfree peasants at the bottom. The kings gave their noblemen gifts and land in return for military support. The aristocracy in turn had ordinary freemen bonded to them by similar ties, and the kin group was of fundamental importance in the regulation of society. From such ties the feudal system of Norman England emerged.

With such a system, it was a relatively easy matter to establish supremacy with a new aristocracy and clergy of Norman French origin. By 1090 only one bishopric was held by an Englishman, and Domesday Book, the inventory of property drawn up in 1086, shows that fewer than six of the 180 major landowners in England were English. The land was mostly held by the King or his Norman French supporters.

On a lower social level, however, additions to the population were not extensive, though there were Norman enclaves in towns such as Nottingham which were effectively separate, with their own by-laws. In all, perhaps about 10,000 Normans entered the country, to mingle with a population of 1.5–2.5 million. There is some suggestion from archaeology, however, that this comparatively small influx may have had an effect on physical appearance in some areas – for instance there are cranial shape changes in the burials at St Helen's-on-the-Wall in York after the Conquest.

The few Norman tenants-in-chief, who received their lands from the King, held territories all over the realm, though their main feudal estates or 'honours' were concentrated in one area. The lands were held in return for units of knight service, that is, they had to supply a certain number of knights for the King's army. The bases of the noblemen were their castles, which they were allowed to fortify only with a licence from the King, and in contrast to Normandy private warfare was successfully repressed in England. Castle building was a prominent feature of the Middle Ages.

Norman government under William was similar to that of Anglo-Saxon England, and the pattern of shires had been established in the ninth century. A council called the King's *Curia Regis* was composed of tenants-in-chief and clergy. It was in essence a court for hearing disputes about land between the tenants-in-chief, modelled on the Anglo-Saxon council of wise men. Local government continued along Anglo-Saxon lines, but bishops and earls ceased to preside over local courts – the former had new ecclesiastical courts, and the latter presided over their honour courts. Under the Normans the jury court became commonplace.

Ill-feeling ran strong over the establishment by the Norman kings of the royal forests (such as the New Forest), since for their creation people were turned out of their homes, and savage penalties were introduced for poaching.

The Normans were succeeded by a line which went back to the counts of Anjou, and it was during this Angevin period chivalry and the concept of courtly love spread from France to England, its dissemination possibly fostered by Eleanor, wife of Henry II (1154–89).

Angevin authority was curbed by the aristocracy, and although their successors the Plantagenets went some way to stabilizing the Crown it was not until the line was ousted by the Tudor Henry VII, who gained power in 1485 and amongst other things confiscated his rivals' lands and wealth, that the power of the nobles was crushed sufficiently for the 'Middle Ages' to develop into the 'Renaissance' of the Tudor period.

Succession Disputes and Warfare

The volatile fortunes of the Crown underlay the instability of the Middle Ages. There were puppet kings, absentee kings, kings who were deposed only to be reinstated after an interlude when a rival reigned, and under-age kings. Women, notably abbesses and the wives of noblemen, could be the pushers and movers in society, but none gained the throne. The many foreign queens brought with them ideas and tastes and commercial links with their homelands as well as the inevitable political alliances. Much of the cultural developments of the period may be traced to such marriage links.

Not all lived up to the chivalric ideal of a Lady (see pp. 37–38). Isabella, wife of Edward II, was probably responsible, with her lover Mortimer, for the murder of her husband.

When Henry I died in 1135, probably of a heart attack, his daughter and designated heir (widow of a Holy Roman Emperor), Matilda, was ignored by Henry's nephew Stephen of Blois who had himself declared King. Matilda landed at Arundel in 1139, capturing castles in the southwest, thus beginning the period known as the Anarchy. She managed to reach London but her arrogance and demands for money lost her support so she was forced in 1148 to retire to Normandy. Thereafter she was a strong influence over her son, Henry II.

The Conquest and the Anarchy, both within the same period of a hundred years, gave the flavour to the entire medieval period in which there was more war than peace.

The Crusades (see p. 14) were a series of eight wars which occurred between 1096 and 1291. Lasting between one and five years each, they were undertaken initially, and ostensibly, to recover the Holy Land from the Muslims, and they had the side-effects of introducing the crusaders to new philosophies and beliefs as well as ways of life. Trade increased and widened.

A period of civil war, known as the Barons' War lasted from 1264 to 1267 (see p. 13) and five years later, its commander was on a crusade when he succeeded to the throne, as Edward I. He immediately put his military expertise to use by embarking on campaigns against the Welsh, the Irish and the Scots.

Wales was Anglicized, control being exercized through a series of castles. Towns were founded, colonized with English merchants and craftsmen, counties were defined, and Welsh law was revised to accord

Stephen penny, 'Watford' type (Lloyd Laing)

with English. Ireland was similarly subdued and Anglicized, being given its own parliament, but the Scots resisted, dealing the English a resounding defeat at Bannockburn in 1314 and finally, with the Treaty of Northampton, coming to an uneasy peace under Robert the Bruce in 1328.

Relationships with France were always volatile during the medieval period (see p. 16). Between 1337 and 1453 the so-called Hundred Years' War with the French distracted attention and funds away from the home front.

Before this was resolved, during the reign of the Lancastrian, Henry VI (1442–71), a struggle began, known as the Wars of the Roses, between the house of Lancaster and that of York. Henry VI succeeded Henry V in infancy in 1422, coming of age in 1442.

The Yorkist Edward IV (who reigned from 1461–70 and 1471–83) took over the throne by force from Henry VI and encountered his strongest opposition from the Earl of Warwick – 'Warwick Kingmaker' – who deposed him with the help of Henry's wife, Margaret of Anjou. From time to time the restored King Henry was paraded before the citizenry of London in old, worn clothes. Edward was forced into exile, returned, recovered the throne, and had Henry disposed of in the Tower of London. (But see also p. 50.)

The Wars of the Roses ended at the battle of Bosworth in 1485 when the Lancastrian Henry VII established himself as King. Through such means as confiscation of his enemies' wealth and marriage to Elisabeth of York, Henry gained sufficient resources to stabilize the monarchy and unite the country. Medieval warfare was closely connected with finance as well as power – prisoners were held for huge ransoms and employment was available for many men.

Government: the King under pressure

The Middle Ages were a period when personality was often paramount, for the barons, given their lands and titles piecemeal by William the Conqueror, were able to build up personal retinues and wealth to rival that of the King. They considered themselves the equals of the King and often acted accordingly. It was the period when history was more often made by the aggressive thug than by the careful administrator. The strength of individual magnates, when united, could and often did overwhelm the monarchy of the day. The result was the slow development of what became the British parliamentary system.

Starting with the reign of King John (1199–1216), a parliament was established that gradually usurped many of the King's powers. When the absentee Richard I was killed during a siege in France he was succeeded by John who did nothing to alleviate the inherited national resentment of the monarchy that had accumulated during the previous two reigns. Church, barons and towns united to curb his powers when he attempted to claim more than his feudal rights, and forced him to agree to the Magna Carta in 1215. This has been seen as some kind of early Declaration of Independence, but in point of fact it was of com-

Newark, Nottinghamshire, episcopal castle mostly of the 12th and 13th centuries, where King John died (Jenny Laing)

paratively little moment, being concerned not with wider liberties but with details of feudal custom.

Conflict, in the form of the Barons' War, continued in the reign of Henry III (1216–72) when it centred on whether the King could appoint his own followers without the consent of the barons. At the forefront of the struggle was Simon de Montfort, who led the opposition. A parliament was summoned in 1258 which led to the drawing up of the Provisions of Oxford which would have made Henry a constitutional monarch had they been successfully maintained. Near Lewes in Sussex, Simon de Montfort captured Henry, his son (later Edward I) and the royalist supporters, forcing the King to agree to the Provisions of Oxford, and a parliament was summoned in his name to which four knights from each shire were called to set up a government that would control the King. In 1265 a second parliament also had representatives of the burgesses of the boroughs as well as knights of the shire. Edward subsequently escaped, and rallied support against Simon de Montfort, who was killed in the ensuing struggle.

De Montfort's supporters were deprived of their lands, but they hid themselves away in forest and fen, and it is to this period, rather than the reign of King John, that the story of Robin Hood may belong (see pp. 33–34).

Popular resistance   The Middle Ages were not a time of democracy. The will of the majority was of no consequence, and only on a handful of occasions did people from the lower echelons make their mark.

Edward II, alabaster effigy, Gloucester Cathedral (National Monuments Record)

One major incident of popular rebellion took place during the reign of Richard II (1377–99). By this time the Poll Tax (originally introduced in the time of Edward III), had been successively and unreasonably modfied. In 1380 a levy of one shilling per head was imposed on the population, with the untenable proviso that the rich should help the poor to pay it. The outcome was the Peasants' Revolt of 1381, led by Wat Tyler. A confrontation in London resulted in the King promising the rebels charters of liberation from serfdom.

Tyler was killed by some of the King's men, and subsequently when the immediate threat was over Richard told the rebels that 'villeins ye are and villeins ye shall remain'.

Although in itself it was a relatively minor rebellion, the Peasants' Revolt did show the peasantry as a force to be reckoned with by landowners. Richard was henceforth seen as a king who wished to be a despot, and he was forced to abdicate, and was imprisoned in Pontefract Castle, Yorkshire, where he died either through suffocation or through self-starvation.

The Crusades

The series of campaigns carried out against the Muslims by Christians intent on capturing Jerusalem are known as the Crusades. The effect in Britain was minimal compared to the rest of Europe, though some unruly elements undoubtedly left, some never to return. Some wealth was lost, but in other cases much was gained. The backing of the Papacy led to greater prestige when things went well, but with the waning of the movement in the late thirteenth century, it suffered inevitable criticism.

During the seventh century the Arab Muslims made extensive conquests in the eastern Mediterranean where the eastern Roman

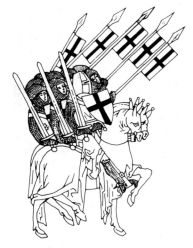

Crusader knights from a manuscript in the British Museum (John Ferguson)

Empire had been ruled from Christian Byzantium (Constantinople). Jerusalem was also sacred to the Muslims. In the eleventh century, Palestine, Syria and Turkey were over-run by Turks who prevented Christian pilgrims entering Palestine. Constantinople was surrounded by Turks, and in 1095 the Byzantine Emperor, Alexius I, appealed to the Pope in Rome. In 1095 at a Council in Clermont the Pope, Urban II, appealed to Christian knights and nobles to free Byzantium and the Holy Land from the Saracens, as the Muslims were termed.

The First Crusade, in 1095 (often called the People's Crusade since it was composed of peasants and tradesmen under the leadership of Peter the Hermit) eventually created a number of Crusader kingdoms including Jerusalem, Tripoli and Edessa.

The Second Crusade was a response to the fall of Edessa in 1144. The Third, which saw the capture of Acre and Cyprus, is significant from the British standpoint in that Richard I (in alliance with Germany and France) was in opposition to the Turkish Sultan Saladin. Richard made peace with Saladin in 1192, the Christians being allowed only a thin coastal strip of Palestine.

The Fourth Crusade is distinguished for the sacking of Constantinople in 1203. Throughout the thirteenth century the Crusader movement waned in popularity, ending when Tripoli and Acre fell. The Children's Crusade of 1212, led by a French shepherd boy of twelve, may be the origin of the legend of the Pied Piper of Hamlyn.

Apart from changes in taste and economic contacts, the Crusades had some effect on developments in the countryside, where manors were established by groups such as the Knights Templar and Hospitaller (see

Banner and red cross of the Knights Templar (John Ferguson, first published in Basic Heraldry *by J. Ferguson and S. Friar, Herbert Press 1993)*

Floor tiles depicting Richard I and Saladin, c.1250–60, Chertsey, Surrey (British Museum)

pp. 100–101). Baldock in Hertfordshire was so named by the Knights Templar who held the manor there, Baldak being Old French for Baghdad.

Politics outside England

In addition to the overseas interest fuelled by the Crusades, relations with France remained volatile throughout the period and the English and Scottish monarchies remained in close contact with the French. Henry II acquired England through his mother, Matilda, and through his marriage to Eleanor of Aquitaine ruled over Normandy, Britanny, Maine, Anjou, Touraine, Poitou, Aquitaine and Gascony. Henry III abandoned Anjou, Normandy and Poitou, but kept the dukedom of Aquitaine and other territories in south-west France. Edward I aspired to reclaim the lost lands, and married his son (Edward II) to the French King's daughter. In 1337 Edward III claimed the French throne, thus beginning the Hundred Years War.

Two major English victories were won at Crécy, in 1346, and at Poitiers in 1356, the latter under Edward the Black Prince (the epithet likely to be a later fanciful one connected with the supposed colour of his armour). The French became demoralized through a complex of circumstances, and in 1360 signed the Treaty of Bretigny by which Edward gave up his claim to the throne of France, but received in return a third of the country, a ransom and the town of Calais. It was during this period that the English started calling the French 'frogs' (because they ate them) and the French started calling the English 'God-damns', for their colourful language. Thus, by 1375 all possessions in France were lost except Calais, Bordeaux and some Breton ports.

Fortunes were reversed however under Henry V, who won control of nearly all of Normandy between 1417 and 1419. He married the daughter of Charles VI of France, and became the heir to the French throne by the terms of the Treaty of Troyes.

English fortunes remained in the ascendant in France until 1428, but in 1436 the tide turned when the English were driven out of Paris. By 1453, only Calais remained in English control.

Scotland

The story of Scotland's 'age of chivalry' begins with David I (1124–53), who was well known in the English court and held lands in England. He introduced Anglo-Norman families to Scotland, including the Bruces of Dumfriesshire and the Stewarts, in Renfrew (who became the Stuart dynasty). Feudalism became well established, and the office of sheriff was introduced. David was also responsible for the development of towns (burghs) in Scotland, and for the reorganization of the Church, with the introduction of claustral monasteries.

David's successor Malcolm IV (1153–65) defeated Somerled, the Viking ruler of Argyll. William the Lion (1165–1214) succeeded in controlling the North, but was captured on a raid into northern England,

Edward III, from his funeral monument, Westminster Abbey (National Monuments Record)

and forced to swear fealty to the English King at the Treaty of Falaise in 1174. His freedom was subsequently bought back.

Alexander II (1214–49) campaigned in Argyll, and was succeeded by Alexander III (1249–86), whose reign was later regarded as a golden age in Scottish history. Alexander's death however led to the Scottish Wars of Independence against Edward I and II. The Treaty of Northampton in 1328 won freedom from England, but its negotiator, Robert I (the Bruce) died the following year.

After the time of Robert the Bruce, unlike Ireland and Wales, Scotland was acknowledged to be a separate entity from England, though the two areas remain inextricably involved in each others' affairs.

Robert's successor, David II (1329–71) has been maligned by historians, but despite renewed war with England he preserved Scottish freedom, though he had been captured at Neville's Cross and ransomed for 100,000 marks.

The reigns of Robert II and Robert III (1371–1406) were dark and troubled times for Scotland, and though James I (1406–37) was a strong ruler, James III (1460–1488) was only six when he succeeded to the throne, and fell foul of the nobles by favouring creative people. He was murdered, fleeing from his opponents at the battle of Sauchieburn.

Despite internal unrest, the fifteenth century was for Scotland a time of prosperity, as it was in England. Burghs flourished, there was an active period of building, and literature was produced.

The Growth of Trade and Towns

The later Middle Ages saw the expansion of overseas trade and the first manifestation of the notion of a nation of shopkeepers rather than food producers.

Although towns did not significantly develop in either Scotland or Wales until after the time of the Norman Conquest, Anglo-Saxon

England already had a well-developed urban network, with a strong pattern of trade and industry and a complex coinage.

The Church

The Norman Conquest accelerated the spread of monasticism, although the process was already underway before the Conquest: in ecclesiastical affairs monastic reforms marked the late Anglo-Saxon period, so that the pattern of dioceses and parishes of the later Middle Ages had been established long before the Norman invasion.

The importance of the Church was paramount. Churchmen, controlled from Rome, entered politics with enthusiasm and often ended up in conflict with the kings. For example, Roger Scrope, Archbishop of York, was beheaded without trial in a barley field for his part in a rebellion which ended in the defeat by Henry IV of the Percy family and the Welsh under Owen Glendower. To the anger of the Archbishop of Canterbury, the elder Percy was quartered and pickled, sections of him being sent to various corners of the realm for public exhibition.

It was not until after the medieval period however, that disputes grew so great that Henry VIII did what many had undoubtedly wished to do before and instituted a total break from the Roman Church.

Disease

When not unsettled by warfare, the population had to contend with disease. The fourteenth century in particular was ravaged by bubonic plague (termed the Black Death in the nineteenth century), which had ultimately originated in China, though outbreaks of plagues, not necessarily bubonic, had occurred before, especially during the Dark Ages. Estimates suggest that between a half and a third of the population succumbed between 1348 and 1349 and the disease continued sporadically in London till the last great plague of 1664–5.

Intellectual and Everyday Life

Intellectual and cultural life, which had recovered after the upheavals of the Dark Ages to flourish in Late Saxon England, was slow to develop in the chaos of political events and the ravages of the Black Death and wars. None the less it is astonishing how much cultural life, how much humour and plain common sense were features of the period, as will be seen in the following chapters.

Folklore

Some of the best-known figures of medieval England are not well-documented historical personnages, but part of folklore. As with all legends, a kernel of truth probably lies behind the myths. Robin Hood (see pp. 33–34), Dick Whittington and King Arthur are three in particular, who along with the concept of chivalry itself have helped to foster the romanticism of the Middle Ages in popular imagination.

ABOVE AND OPPOSITE: *details of early 13c windows from Canterbury Cathedral (Patrick Reyntiens, first published in* The Beauty of Stained Glass, *Herbert Press 1990)*

Dick Whittington Dick Whittington, hero of Christmas pantomimes, was born in March 1423, the son of a Gloucestershire knight who went to London where he opened a mercer's shop. His customers included Henry Bolingbroke (later Henry IV). He became an active figure in London politics, and served as Lord Mayor three times, in 1397–98, 1406–07 and 1419–20.

His personal wealth was considerable, and both Henry IV and Henry V borrowed from him. He bequeathed his fortune to charity, including the foundation of a college for priests and an almshouse.

Dick Whittington, 'thrice Lord Mayor of London', then, was historical fact. The story of his cat is however apocryphal, and was not recorded until 1605.

King Arthur sits dejectedly after returning Excalibur to the lake. 14C drawing, from Le Roman de Lancelot du Lac et de la Mort du Roi Artu, *MS Add. 10294, f. 94 (British Library)*

King Arthur King Arthur is a shadowy figure about whom almost nothing is known, though a number of references in sources relating back to the fifth/sixth century have led modern scholars to believe that he was a Romano-British leader in south-west England who fought the Anglo-Saxons. The king who was married to queen Guinevere and presided over the Round Table with his knights such as Lancelot and Bedevere is a medieval fiction which was of political significance.

He grew in stature following a visit made by the librarian of Malmesbury Abbey (Wiltshire), to some of his fellow Benedictines at Glastonbury. Through the librarian's patron, the Earl of Gloucester, the story that Arthur was buried at Glastonbury reached the ears of Geoffrey of Monmouth, who wrote about Arthur in his *History of the Kings of Britain*. This account was largely fiction, but it did not prevent Henry II naming his grandson Arthur in 1187 in the (vain) hope that as Arthur II he would unite England, for the Normans and Angevins were sensitive about their claim to England.

The concept of an Arthur II might have been acceptable in England, but the Welsh were outraged since they regarded the legendary king as a fellow-countryman who was asleep under Snowdon until he should be needed. To put an end to this claim it was politically essential that the real Arthur had to be found and shown to be dead.

When, conveniently for this aim, the abbey was burned down in 1190, the clearance revealed Arthur's tomb. The coffin was found to contain the body of a tall man with damaged skull, and the bones of a smaller person, with, poignantly, a lock of golden hair that fell to pieces when touched by a monk. The remains were reburied, and would have remained at peace had another political crisis not arisen. When Edward I was planning his campaign in Wales it was deemed politically correct to re-assert that Arthur was dead and buried in England, and so the remains were dug up again, the skulls removed 'for the veneration of the people', and the bodies reburied at Glastonbury.

Henceforth the myth of Arthur and his knights was increasingly embroidered. The stories were taken up in France, where Chrétien de Troyes began to elaborate upon them. The whole cycle crystallized into a heroic saga by Mallory, whose *Morte d'Arthur* gained even wider currency through being one of the first books printed in English, by Caxton.

There is no doubt that it was believed that the bodies disinterred by Henry II and Edward I were those of Arthur and Guinevere. The grave was re-excavated in 1962 and, not surprisingly, found to be empty.

The sixteenth-century antiquary William Camden sketched a lead cross that was supposed to have been found when Arthur's grave was opened. It was inscribed,

HIC IACET SEPULTUS INCLITUS REX ARTURIUS
IN INSULA AVALONIA

'Here lies buried the famous King Arthur in the Isle of Avalon'.

There is no doubt about the authenticity of the cross – it came to light again recently before being 'lost' again. The style of the lettering is in keeping with the tenth century, and could have been made on the orders of St Dunstan, who may have had the original grave moved during building works at that time. The form of the inscription has echoes of a genuine sixth-century formula, which perhaps read,

HIC IACIT ARTURIUS SEPULTUS IN HOC TUMULO

This might have been inscribed on Arthur's original tombstone.

Sources

With the possible exception of the fifteenth century, which is less well documented than preceding periods, the Middle Ages are well chronicled in a wealth of written documents, many of which still remain to be fully assessed.

The lost Glastonbury Cross, apparently put on Arthur's grave by late Saxon monks. Drawing by William Camden from his Britannia, *1607*

The Garden of Love, from Roman de la Rose, *MS Harl. 4425, f. 12 (British Library)*

OPPOSITE: *Armorials, drawn by Matthew Paris, mid 13C MS Nero D1, f. 171 verso (British Library)*

England is particularly rich in documentary sources for towns and town life in the Middle Ages, though the bulk of the information relates to the period after 1300. For the situation at the time of the Norman Conquest, Domesday book, compiled in 1086, provides valuable information, while the twelfth and thirteenth centuries are documented in state archives, such as the Pipe Rolls, The Patent Rolls, the Close Rolls and the Fine Rolls. From the fourteenth century onwards many towns have surviving records of their own, such as property transactions, wills and charters, and documents which relate to urban upkeep. There is also a body of documentary sources for churches and church holdings in towns. Ports in particular, such as Southampton, King's Lynn, Hull, and of course London, are rich in documentation of the trade that passed through them.

Urban archaeology is a comparatively new study, accelerated by the rebuilding programmes in cities that followed bomb damage in World War II, and subsequently the large-scale civic building programmes that marked the sixties and seventies, but which have subsequently slowed down. London was one of the first cities to receive the serious attention of archaeologists as a prelude to rebuilding, but Leicester, Exeter and Canterbury to name but three also saw some early post-War work. Since the major excavation programmes of the 1960s and 1970s at Winchester, Southampton, Oxford, Stamford, King's Lynn, Lincoln, Gloucester and York, to name but a few towns, the scale of archaeological excavation has been reduced, but important work continues to be done. Much of the archaeological excavation work tends to be 'rescue' operations in advance of building, with the result that information has been recovered in a somewhat piecemeal fashion. However, through the active collaboration between archaeologists and historians, an understanding of town development is continuing to increase very rapidly.

In the countryside, similar written records (for example the Manorial Rolls) exist in smaller numbers and archaeological methods which are particularly vital in this context include aerial photography and dendrochronology (a method of dating wood).

The study of deserted medieval villlages (DMVs, see p. 79) has escalated since the 1940s and has greatly increased our knowledge of the lives of the vast majority of the population who were neither literate nor the subject of written records. A relatively recent development has been church archaeology.

Certain sites occur more frequently than others in this text — for example, Caerlaverock, Nottingham, Southampton and York. This is simply a reflection of available material for illustration or the amount of study completed by scholars and does not indicate any particular prominence during the medieval period.

1 · Society

OVERLEAF: *Caernarvon Castle, Gwynedd, interior showing curtain wall and towers. Begun by Edward I for his Welsh campaigns, 1283–1330 (Philip Dixon)*

THE CONCEPT of being born into a place in society underscored much of medieval life, which revolved around land ownership and duties owed to other people. The role of women within the social order was ambivalent.

With the establishment of Norman overlords a yawning gap opened between the land-owning minority and the rest of society.

Knights

The knights were the military supporters of the feudal lords. The knight fought for his lord and when necessary died for him.

But the feudal inheritance provided only for the eldest son. Younger sons tended therefore to go into the church or to join the groups of landless knights, waiting at court for their opportunity to marry into an estate.

It was not essential to hold a fief (property or service fee) to be a knight, and the court was full of knights bachelor, who were in essence apprentice knights. The pressure on younger sons to enter the Church meant that there were many churchmen little suited to their calling (forced celibacy might well account for the diatribes against women which have had repercussions to the present day). Some clergy even bore arms, though this became increasingly rare as time wore on.

There were three methods of becoming a knight – the commonest involved the King or a tenant-in-chief conferring the title, known as 'dubbing'. A second method had stronger religious undertones: the knight-to-be kept vigil all through the night with his arms on the altar in front of him. He then took a purifying bath, heard Mass and had his spurs put on. There followed the dubbing with a sword and a formal sermon.

The third method was entirely clerical, and involved the reading of a service, *Benedictio Novi Militis*.

A type of apprenticeship for knighthood was served through being a squire, which involved acting as a servant in a noble household while being instructed in manners, humility and various skills.

Knighthood was co-optive; in essence, it was a military guild which maintained strict class divisions. It has been pointed out that the knightly class could only exist if there were also churls.

After the battles of Crécy and Poitiers the French knights who had been taken prisoner were treated as guests. This is well exemplified by the way in which, while John of Gaunt (Duke of Lancaster and head of government during the latter years of Edward III and the minority

of Richard II) and the King of Portugal were fighting against the French, famine and dysentry broke out among the English ranks. The sick knights were given safe conduct to convalesce among the French (to the horror of the King of Portugal, who saw them as deserters). Once suitably recovered, they returned to the other side to continue fighting.

Chivalric manners Around the military training of a knight an accretion of manners and customs grew up which is conveniently grouped as 'chivalry'. Part of this was the cultivation of courtly manners, an idea initially derived (like many other things) from the Saracens encountered on the Crusades, but developed particularly in France in the twelfth century and transmitted to England. Then, as now, one of the main functions of 'manners' was to separate the fashionable from the uncouth. The chivalric code furthered an idea of social service without remuneration, and ideas of loyalty, virtue and generosity. It fostered *noblesse oblige* – privileges which carried with them responsibilities.

In respect of manners, the worst offenders against courtly behaviour appear to have been the Germans – John of Salisbury recorded how Roger II of Sicily welcomed all foreigners to his court except Germans, 'on account of their extreme barbarousness'.

Alongside the cult of courtly manners grew up the idea of romantic love and the chivalrous devotion of a knight to his lady (see pp. 37–38).

By the fourteenth century chivalry was in decline.

Society in the Countryside

Mail shirt (habergeon), probably 14C (Museum of London)

Fundamental to the feudal structure was the concept of the manor, which released knights from work on their farms to fight for the King. Work was carried out on the manor by the tenants, who held lands from the lord and were given his protection in return for service on his demesne land (i.e. land owned and occupied by the lord). The manor was in theory a village, but in fact was more an abstraction which meant different things in different places – some manors comprised several villages, some several farms; in some cases there were several manors in a village.

In theory too, a manor had a manorial hall and court, but some villages had no manorial hall at all and some comprised nothing but demesne land, where all holdings were the King's.

By the thirteenth century tenants often paid more in money rents than in services.

Villeins made up the main element in the village population. They swore fealty to their lord, and enjoyed no rights under common law – the lord could evict them from their fields, increase rents or impose tallage (tax) on them as he saw fit. Despite this, they could become successful farmers in their own right, holding between ten and forty acres. Their lack of freedom however was a major stigma, and in 1300 a manorial court fined a villager who accused his neighbours in public of being 'villeins'.

Late 13C aquamanile (water container) in the shape of a knight, copper alloy, from the Tyne near Hexham (British Museum)

Below villeins were cottars, who held no more than five acres, and whose dues to the lord were different. A cottar might work as plough-man for his lord, in return for the right to use his lord's plough and team on a Saturday, for example.

The peasant farmer owned little. An inventory for one at Trumpington, Cambridge, lists his belongings as 'a hoe, a spade, an axe, a bill-hook, two yokes for buckets and a barrel,' the collective value of which was set at 10d.

Superior to villeins were freemen. Legal free status did not necessarily mean superior wealth — a rich villein could employ a poor freeman. Their dues to the lord however tended to be of a more administrative order — they organized villeins and cottars in their services, for example.

In 1247 freemen who had extensive holdings (land worth forty shillings a year) were knighted, to enable them to work in shire courts. In the late Middle Ages such freemen were known as yeomen.

Inheritance To protect his family and the land the position of a knight was often hereditary, for life could be short, and the overlord

*Bodiam, East Sussex, late 14C
quadrangular castle with moat
(Philip Dixon)*

*Pot, possibly used as a 'bomb', one
of many identical from the moat,
Caerlaverock, Dumfriesshire
(Historic Scotland)*

Armour piercing arrow, with part of the original wooden shaft, from the wet moat, Caerlaverock Castle, Dumfriesshire (Historic Scotland)

who did not continue to support the knight's successor was despised by all. Inheritance of rights in the land was usually by the eldest son, but sometimes the youngest son inherited on the argument that the eldest was better able to look after himself; the customs of inheritance varied considerably from region to region. Either way, many were left without their own holdings – some worked on their brother's land, others went to the towns or went to war or on crusades.

Villeins did not normally marry until they had inherited (usually in their late twenties), unlike the nobility, who married young.

Social mobility   The life of serfs was not entirely without possibility of escape however. A cottar could acquire freedom by paying his lord a 'fine'. So might a villein, but it was harder, paradoxically, for him, since the 'fine' was that much higher.

A runaway could gain freedom if he managed to hide himself on the demesne lands of the king or in a chartered town for a year and a day, and a villein could become free by marrying a free woman.

With the development of trade and town life towards the end of the Middle Ages, the beginnings of a new middle class, based on commerce, grew up as escape to the towns to find work increased.

Part of this process would have been gradual since many farmers were also craftsmen, though the amount of farming carried out by citizens varied markedly from town to town.

Leicester, Coventry and Gloucester to name but three were towns in which farming was still an important element in the economy at this date. In others, such as Canterbury and Norwich, farming was of minimal importance.

Other methods of living outside the legal stranglehold of feudal society developed by the end of the Middle Ages, for example by Elizabethan times beggars were a prominent menace.

From the fifteenth century on, the gypsies (the word comes from Egyptians since they falsely represented themselves as such) arrived in western Europe after some four centuries of wandering from their Indian homelands.

Peasant removing a thorn from foot. Early 13c carving on a capital in Wells Cathedral (The Dean and Chapter of Wells)

Robin Hood

There was also a place in society for outlaws, of whom Robin Hood is the most famous.

The story of Robin Hood is one of the most enduring traditions in English folklore, and for many symbolizes medieval England. Tracing the origins of the legend however is a complex matter, partly because the name of Robin Hode or Hood is not uncommon in the Middle Ages.

Robin Hood — illustration from
A Lytrell Geste of Robyn
Hode, *c.1490*

He first figures in English ballads, composed probably in the earlier fourteenth century, and in William Langland's *Piers Ploughman* (1377) in which there is the line 'I can [know] rymes of Robin Hode and Randle Erle of Chestre', spoken by a drunken chaplain. By the late fifteenth century the select band of the 'merry men' was growing; 1475 saw the first mention of Friar Tuck in print and in 1500 Maid Marian was mentioned in the *Ship of Fools* by Alexander Barclay. Thereafter literary accounts differ in their claims as to when and where Robin Hood lived.

An anonymous chronicle in the Sloane manuscripts in the British Museum states that Robin was born in about 1160 in Locksley in Yorkshire or Nottinghamshire, a claim which lacks credence since there is no such place in either county (though there is one in Staffordshire).

The suggestion that Robin was active in the time of Richard I was not made until 1521, and it was not until 1795 that Robin was placed in Nottinghamshire, a claim made in a two-volume study by the antiquary Joseph Ritson who suggested Robin had lived in the time of Henry II.

Separate traditions place Robin in Yorkshire, in the time of Edward II or in Nottingham in the time of King John.

The Yorkshire Robin is the more credible as an historical figure. The birth of a Robert Hode is documented in Wakefield around 1290, and there are records of how he married a certain Matilda and lived in a five-roomed house. Thomas, Earl of Lancaster, called this Robin to fight at the Battle of Boroughbridge, from which he escaped to hide in the neighbouring forest. Yorkshire tradition suggests that he was later pardoned by Edward II, and went into service with the King, before returning to his old haunts. The domestic accounts of Edward II show that on November 22 the King ordered that Robin Hood be given five shillings 'because he can no longer work here'.

Men and Women in Medieval Society

The relationship between men and women in the Middle Ages remained in many respects unchanged until the women's movements of the twentieth century. Views of women were confused and their standards of living and level of independence could vary considerably from the very poorest to the richest. On the one hand misogynists did their utmost to denigrate and relegate them to the role of slaves and baby factories. On the other, in a direct attempt, notably by men, to redress the balance, ideas of chivalry elevated them to objects of worship. Affected by, but probably very little connected with, either of these views were the real medieval women who were generally treated with reasonable respect. Certainly at least some were able to attain positions of importance and economic power in the workplace as well as in the home. Even the Church eventually found itself unable to maintain a united anti-female front.

The concept of freedom of speech for the vast majority of females in particular, was non-existent:

It is ordained by common assent that all the women of the township control their tongues without any sort of defamation.

This declaration is to be found in the Durham Rolls, in connection with a court case involving a man and wife:

From Agnes of Ingleby – for transgression against William Sparrow and Gillian his wife, calling the said Gillian a harlot, to the damage of £2 whence they will take at their will 13s 4d; as was found by the jury – by way of penalty and fine 3s 4d; reduced in mercy to 6d.

Loose tongues were a constant problem in the middle ages when gossip was regarded as a particularly deadly sin. Women were singled out for punishments in this area to the point where the English court-rolls refer to numerous villages fined or threatened with fines for failing to have cucking stools for scolds (for ducking them in ponds). Iron headpieces called scolds' bridles were another method of curbing freedom of female speech. Chaucer's tale of Patient Griselde extolls the virtues of fortitude in the face of gross injustice, which, in the end pays off for the hapless wife.

The Ecclesiastical View of Women   The relegation of women to inferior status began early in the Church. Clerics put forward a partisan viewpoint which with the passage of time became exaggeratedly influential for the simple reason that they constituted the majority of literate members of society, or were their teachers. The importance and influence of the Church in medieval and later society must not be underestimated.

St Paul consigned women to a secondary status, an attitude which was fostered by St Augustine and other early fathers of the Church. The authority for this stand was nothing less than the book of Genesis, in which God informs Eve,

I will greatly multiply thy sorrow and thy conception, in sorrow thou shalt bring forth children, and thy desire shall be to thy husband, and he shall rule over thee, (Gen. 3, 16).

To Tertullian, writing in the late second/early third century, women were the 'devil's gateway' and a 'temple built over a sewer'. Later still, St John Chrysotom claimed they were, 'phlegm, blood, bile, rheum and the fluids of digested food ... behind ... a whitened sepulchre'.

For such reasons, women were seen as being subject to all the temptations the devil had to offer, particularly those of the flesh. They were punished for eternity by such afflictions as the menstrual cycle and the pain of childbirth. Even the bodies of women were seen to be a blundered form of the ideal, for the male genitals were formed outside the body, the female squeezed shamefully inside.

in the woman for sothe in the stede of the yarde [penis] ys the necke of the moder[womb] ... and yr hath small balokkys, netheles brode ...

It followed logically therefore to consider:

the necke of yr in comparycon to the ballokkys ys in maner of a yerd or a pyntyl y-turned inwarde (quoted in Carole Rawcliffe, *Medicine and Society in Later Medieval England*, Stroud, 1995, 174).

Women, according to certain medieval men, eagerly pre-empting the twentieth century concept of penis envy, liked sex because it gave them a penis, if only briefly.

For those whose understanding of sex was less than it might be, help could be sought during the later Middle Ages in the form of a sex manual called *Secrets of Women*. Amongst other things, this earnestly explained that women were,

venomous during the time of their flowers [periods] and so very dangerous that they poison beasts with their glance and little children in their cots, sully and stain mirrors, and on some occasions those men who lie with them in carnal intercourse are made leprous (Rowland, B. (ed.) *Medieval Woman's Guide to Health*, Kent, Ohio, 1981, 58–9).

It was also held that for conception, semen had to be produced by the ovaries. Thus it was assumed that if a child were conceived as the outcome of a rape, the woman must have responded willingly. However, another school of thought considered that conception was entirely due to the male, and that the womb was an empty vessel in which the implanted child might grow.

Ecclesiastical diatribes against women undoubtedly had a lasting and detrimental effect on their well-being.

Secular mysogyny Anti-female feelings were also expressed in secular circles. There was a thriving literary tradition about perfidious women, known in France as *fabliaux*.

The Wife of Bath in Chaucer's *Canterbury Tales* was a feminist well ahead of her time, who complained about having to listen to her fifth husband droning on from his book of 'wikked wyves' about men betrayed by women – such as Samson, Hercules, Agamemnon and Socrates (who had a shrewish wife, Xantippe).

'For trusteth well,' proclaimed the Wife of Bath, 'it is an impossible that any clerk will speak good of wives', adding that 'By God, if women had written stories, they would have written of men more wickedness than all the mark of Adam may redress!'.

Chaucer compiled a work called the *Legend of Good Women*, and not surprisingly, the Wife of Bath was not alone among women who fought back against the tide of vitriol: some women may have been the originators of many of the pro-women writings. Perhaps one composed the anonymous fifteenth-century poem which includes the following critical lines which are none the less overly fatalistic to modern ears:

> A woman is a worthy thyng
> They do the wash and do the wrynge
> Lullay, Lullay, she doth the synge
> And yet she has but care and woo.

A woman is a worthy wyght
She serveth a man both daye and nyght,
Thereto she puttyth all her myght,
And yet she hathe but care and woo.

The romantic ideal – chivalry and women   To counter the concept of women as the empty vessels of Satan, the medieval world came up with the ideal of romantic love and chivalry. By the twelfth century men were increasingly realizing that the female workload and other burdens were exceptionally heavy, and that women deserved greater respect than the Church accorded them.

Women, too, seem to have been increasingly assertive and outwardgoing. In France, where chivalry was born, Guilbert, abbot of Nogent lamented,

maidenly modesty and honour have fallen off, and the mother's care decayed, so that nothing can be seen in them but unseemly mirth, the noise of jokes, with winking eyes and babbling tongues, and wanton gait, and most ridiculous manners. The quality of their garments is unlike the simplicity of the past; in the widening of their sleeves, the tightness of the bodice – nay, in the whole person – we may see how shame is cast aside.

The new factor which entered the twelfth century scene was the recognition of sexuality. *Ars Amoris* (the Art of Love), written by Ovid (43 BC to AD 17), became popular reading in courtly circles.

His tongue-in-cheek directives for seduction were taken up by the troubadours of southern France, where the Church was corrupt and less respected than in other areas of Europe. The clergy were seen to marry and keep mistresses even as they preached sexual abstinence.

Due to wars and other factors, there were many knights without property, and many ladies without husbands. The physical and emotional needs of both might be met without recourse to marriage.

In twelfth-century France, there was nothing platonic about courtly love. 'May God grant that I live long enough to have my hands beneath her cloak', wrote William of Poitiers of one beloved, and again, as directly, 'How many times did I tumble them? A hundred-and-eighty-eight to be precise, so that I almost broke my girth and harness'.

Other troubadours were equally forthright, but as time progressed the concept of courtly love developed out of simple lust, perhaps transformed through the influence of Moorish literature such as Ali ibn Hazm's *The Dove's Neck-Ring* which was written in the early eleventh century and elevated the more spiritual side of love (though physical desire was not forgotten).

In this kind of love, the lover was ennobled, and was jealous and abject before his beloved. The greatest joy of love was to be found in the misery of the smitten male, awaiting the slightest feminine kindness to elevate him to supreme elation.

With the Moorish concept of romantic love came also the idea of codes of chivalrous behaviour. For the Moors, however, courtly love

Brass effigy of Sir Robert de Bures from the church of All Saints, Acton, Suffolk (Clark Paterson [Brass Rubbings] Ltd)

was something that should only happen between the unattached. When the idea reached the West it was modified to focus upon the wives of other men, for in chivalric society it was inconceivable that a man might be in love with his wife, however fond he might be of her. Indeed, some theologians actually stated that passionate love by a man for his own wife was adultery.

On to the modified Moorish doctrine were grafted elements borrowed directly from Ovid.

The key elements in romantic love were all fundamentals of feudal society. The courteous behaviour required stemmed from the pattern which had evolved in the development of the feudal relationship between king and vassal. The humility necessary in a lover was paralleled in the humility of the vassal before his lord – the lover was the emotional vassal of his lady.

For romantic love to work it took two to play, and there was no shortage of partners. The social gulf was often enormous and did not seem to trouble either side.

Thus far the stage had been mostly southern France. The flag of courtly love was brought north to England by Eleanor of Aquitaine, who married Henry II in 1154 (having previously been married to Louis of France). The literary tradition of romantic poetry which was prevalent in her native Languedoc was introduced first to northern France (notably Rouen and Troyes), and then London. In the fullness of time Eleanor went to Poitiers where she established her own court which constituted a kind of feudal 'fun set'.

It was in this court that Chrétien de Troyes penned his Arthurian tales. His early poem *Erec* predates chivalric romance but the arrival in Troyes of Marie of Champagne, Eleanor's eldest daughter, changed his outlook, and under her guidance at Poitiers he wrote in verse the story of *Lancelot*, the archetypal model for all successful yarns of romantic, adulterous love.

Marie of Champagne was responsible for another landmark in the development of romantic love. Her chaplain, Andreas Capellanus, was (rather improbably, given the Church's views) asked to write a book called *The Art of Courtly Love*. For there to be love, he decided, the participants had to be of the right social class. While he conceded that even serfs might sometimes feel a stirring in their loins, ('like any horse or mule'), the 'uninterrupted solace of plough and mattock' would soon sort them out. He added also that jealousy was an important spice in any liaison.

The Cult of the Virgin   The Church was not totally untouched by the spirit of the times, however, and there rapidly developed a cult of the Virgin Mary. While it is true that many churchmen were bigotted, others were logical, critical thinkers, so the denigration of women had posed real problems for some medieval theologians. One writer commented,

Woman is to be preferred to man, to wit in material: Adam made from clay and Eve from side of Adam; in place: Adam made outside paradise and Eve w'in; in conception: a woman conceived God which a man did not do; in apparition: Christ appeared to a woman after the Resurrection, to wit the Magdalene; in exaltation: a woman is exalted above the choirs of angels, to wit the Blessed Mary.

St Bernadine even declared that:

It is a great grace to be a woman: more women are saved than men. (Quoted in Power, E. *Medieval Women*, Cambridge, (1975), 14).

It is notable that the cult of the Virgin Mary was in the ascendant even before the concept of chivalric love gained impetus. Current in the eleventh century, it dominated the whole of the medieval period. Pilgrimages were made to shrines dedicated to the Virgin at Walsingham, Ipswich and elsewhere: wild flowers were named after her (e.g. Virgin's Bower): churches were furnished with Lady Chapels throughout the land, and the image of the Virgin was to be seen everywhere. Saturdays were dedicated to her worship. The veneration of the Virgin came close to that found in chivalric love.

Between them, courtly love and the cult of the Virgin marked the first stage in the process of putting women on a pedestal that prevailed in Europe for the next eight hundred years. In turn it caused limitations to women's independence and well-being. None the less, although the cult of the Virgin may have pervaded all ranks of society, the exaltation of women as a whole was largely confined to the upper social echelons.

Differing attitudes to women in Europe   Social patterns in medieval England were at some variance to those in the Mediterannean, where women married young, and arranged marriage was common. In England, many women did not marry until their mid twenties, and prior to that they worked, usually in service, even in cases where they later became mistresses of households themselves. In north-west Europe there was a greater emphasis on late 'companionate' marriage, and (with shades of modern thinking) on mutual affection. Northern European pastoral manuals (books for priests giving practical advice on how to tend their parishoners) address such subjects as maternal care, sexual double standards and prostitution. In contrast, Mediterranean concerns were much more with marriage brokers and issues such as the canonical minimum age for marriage and rules regarding whether the couple were related within the permitted degrees of consanguinity.

Women at work   Medieval women were not purely housewives. In the upper social ranks, they had to understand their husbands' work, in order to take over running the estates or businesses when the men were absent, perhaps at war. In the fifteenth century it has been estimated that 76 per cent of noble houses were reduced by at least one third for, on average, a period of seventeen years.

Widows often continued their husbands' work. Then as now, women worked to supplement the family income, or, if they were not

Brass effigy of Sir Robert de Setvans from the church of St Mary, Chartham, Kent (Clark Paterson [Brass Rubbings] Ltd)

married, to provide themselves with a livelihood, for women in the Middle Ages outnumbered available men, whose numbers were probably drastically depleted by endemic warfare or possibly the priesthood.

Women usually assisted their husbands if they were craftsmen, or took up their own craft. Some guilds excluded women, with the exception of the wives and daughters of the guild members, and others made special provision for widows carrying on their husbands' craft. In London the widows of freemen were made freewomen of the city.

In the later fourteenth and fifteenth centuries many young people of both sexes found jobs in towns, and met their future spouses in the workplace. They were married with their employers' blessings.

In the country it was more difficult for young women to move outside their own local circle to find partners, and many daughters of prosperous farmers remained at home and were more subject to social pressures in choice of a spouse.

Although most activities were engaged in by both men and women, some attracted more women. A study of Alrewas in Derbyshire has shown that in this rural manor at any rate there was some division of labour according to sex. Women were mostly involved in brewing, while men engaged in other agricultural pursuits.

Women could be apprenticed to trades in the way that men were. In 1407 a statute forbade those who did not possess an annual rent of twenty shillings per annum from apprenticing a son or daughter to a trade. Although girls were sometimes apprenticed to men, they were usually apprenticed to the wives, and initiation into a trade could begin very early, with tiny children helping their mothers to sort and card wool for spinning, for example. In fourteenth century London, William Brewer of Holborn and his wife Elena were taken before the court for having apprenticed a girl at the age of three who worked for them for seven years before returning to her parents.

In 1388 the Statute of Labourers forbade boys and girls who had been employed in agriculture to the age of twelve from being apprenticed in a trade.

Women did not always follow their husbands' trade, however, but were often free to pursue one of their own. Women could for example be found working as butchers, chandlers, ironmongers, net-makers, cobblers, glovers, girdlers, haberdashers, purse-makers, cup-makers, skinners, bookbinders, gilders, painters, silk weavers, embroiderers, spicers, smiths and goldsmiths. The Poll Tax returns for the West Riding of Yorkshire in the last quarter of the fourteenth century give a range of jobs done by women, and in which proportions: 6 pedlars; 39 brewsters; 11 innkeepers; 2 farmers; 1 farrier; 1 smith; 1 shoe maker; 1 merchant; 22 nurses and 114 domestic or farm servants. These are, of course, only those whose occupations are given.

Then, as now, women tended to be more badly paid than men for the same work, and there was a constant hostility to women from the men in the workplace lest they were undercut.

The industries most popular with women were those that could be undertaken at home, notably the textile industries and those concerned with food and drink, such as brewing and baking. Many women seem to have combined one or two crafts, notably in the countryside where there were no guilds to which they might belong.

Unmarried women were most often employed in spinning, hence the derivation of the word 'spinster'.

Married or not, many women worked in sales – the medieval term was *regrater*. But the women were as capable of sharp practice as their male counterparts:

But to say the truth in this instance the trade of regratery belongeth by right the rather to women. For if a woman be at it she in her stinginess useth much moire machination and deceit than a man; for never alloweth she the profit on a single crumb to escape her, nor faileth to hold her neighbour to paying his price. (John Gower, *Mirour de l'Omme,* late fourteenth century, quoted in Power, E. *Medieval Women*, Cambridge, 1975, 68).

When not engaged in making money, women were supposed to be charitable, and were expected by their husbands as an extension of household responsibility to give fuel and sometimes shelter for the poor. They also initiated charitable projects, or undertook them with their spouses.

Love and Marriage

By around 1300, English pastoral manuals began to emphasize the importance of marital love. The text of the marriage service includes:

Note according to the Master [Peter Lombard] in the fourth [book] of the Sentences, Eve was made from man's side, not from another part, for this reason: to show that she was created in a society of love – lest, if she had by chance been made from the man's head, she should have seemed to be brought forth for domination, or, if made from his feet, brought forth in order to suffer servitude. From which it appears that a wife is not to be honoured by her husband like a lady, nor to be treated vielly like a hand-made, but really loved as a companion.

This sort of attitude arose no doubt in response to the fact that some men felt affection for their wives despite the Church's views. Richard II, for example, who married Anne of Bohemia for political reasons in 1382, became fond of her with the passage of time. When she died, he demolished her favourite palace, because it reminded him of her, and knocked down the Earl of Arundel at her funeral for arriving late.

Marriages were dictated by economic factors, and as many of the population died young, marriages were often short and second marriages about as common as they are in western society today.

Marriage was essentially a civil contract in the earlier Middle Ages, though increasingly the Church involved itself in the arrangement. By the thirteenth century the custom of a church wedding become com-

Adam and Eve on a font at East Meon, Hants (Philip Dixon)

mon, but marriage was not made a sacrament until 1439. Even then, the public plighting of troths was considered the more important ceremony.

In the civil ceremony, the important element was the dowry. In the higher echelons of society, marriages were arranged for dynastic and financial gain, and marriage to someone of a lower rank was held in contempt. When the seventeen-year-old Margery Paston fell in love with her parents' estate bailiff, Richard Calle, and secretly married him in 1466, her mother refused to speak to her again. Although Calle was allowed to keep his job, the parents continued to treat him as a bailiff, not a son-in-law.

Marriages without approval could happen on any level. Marjorie, Countess of Carrick, is said to have kidnapped Robert Bruce in the 1270s in order to marry him. This did not suit Alexander III, the then King of Scotland, who seized several of her estates in vengeance. The Church however supported the union, and they stayed together, their son being the Scottish patriot, Robert the Bruce.

A mutual promise to marry, made before witnesses, was sufficient to make a marriage binding, and the Church found itself upholding such impromtu weddings despite parental approbation.

Then as always, whether the marriage was for financial or dynastic reasons or for love, sometimes it worked out and sometimes it did not.

Divorce was expensive, for it required papal approval, thus effectively barring it from the majority of the population. However, annulment was more common and it was possible, for example, for a man to 'discover' that he was related to his wife, thus becoming eligible for annulment.

Contraception   Many manuals are much concerned with the avoidance of conception. They include 'poisons of sterility' which in some cases at least appear to have been something to drink: a concoction of rosemary, balsam and/or parsley was deemed particularly effective.

Failing that, there were more practical contraceptives, such as the

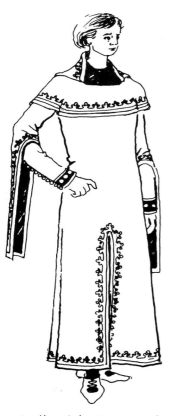

A nobleman's dress from c.1350 (Joan Nunn, first published in Fashion in Costume 1200–1980, *Herbert Press 1994)*

use of beeswax or cloth to impede the journey of the semen. Cheaper but undoubtedly more precarious was simply holding the breath.

There were moral debates about whether it was permissible to prevent conception if it were known that the ensuing childbirth would result in death. Abortions were sometimes induced – 'douching' and eating lead were two methods, though less drastic was the consumption of myrrh and coriander.

Unrespectable liaisons Although the Church regarded celibacy as the ideal state, it was not until the thirteenth century that penalties were invented for fornication and adultery.

Of course, even among the clergy, hypocrisy was rife. Some parishes felt it advisable to force their priests to marry, in order to protect the local wives and daughters. The vicar of Brent Eleigh was described as a 'common ravisher of wives and virgins' when he stood before the court for raping a Margaret Webbe in 1401.

Although we do not have any figures for Britain, statistics for the composition of the clientele of a brothel at Dijon in the Middle Ages showed that 20 per cent were clerics, and the situation was probably little different in England. Many priests got round their problems by employing 'housekeepers'.

Homosexuality posed a problem for the Church since it held that there was no such thing as a homosexual – only a heterosexual who indulged in perverted practices. During the twelfth century a homosexual culture flourished in many monasteries, but later in the Middle Ages as penalties became stricter it was kept more under wraps.

The fate of Edward II (1307–27), who died at the hands of his magnates, was directly connected with his sexuality. A mild-mannered, alleged homosexual who enjoyed swimming, theatricals and physical exercise, he was the son of the military campaigner, Edward I (see p. 11). He was charged with breaking his coronation oath, forced to abdicate and imprisoned, first in Kenilworth Castle then in Berkeley Castle. Attempts to free him failed, and it was announced that he had died peacefully, of natural causes, in 1327. Traditionally he died by having a 'hoote broche putte thro' the secret place posteriale', so that there would be no obvious signs on the corpse of how he had died.

The Church took a long time to make up its mind about lesbianism, which was found particularly in nunneries. The initial line was that it was no great sin, and best left unmentioned, but by the late tenth/early eleventh century a dimmer view was being taken by clerics such as Burchard of Worms, who demanded a whole year's penance for lesbian women, with a further two years for women who had used sexual aids in group sessions. Monks who used sexual aids had a mere forty days' penance.

In the thirteenth century Matthew Paris narrated a tale of a 'good-looking noblewoman [who] ... impregnated another woman ... and in some weird and wonderful way became a father.' (Bear in mind that medieval women produced semen – see p. 36.)

Entering a nunnery was not necessarily occasioned by genuine piety and nuns did not only develop intra-mural passions. Among documented cases of errant nuns, mention may be made of Margaret Wavere, who was prioress of Catesby and was charged not only with pawning church silver, but with allowing frequent visits from her lover, a priest called William Taylour. Chaucer's Prioress had a brooch inscribed 'Love Conquers All' and, with her courtly manners was clearly a recognizable type for the readers of the *Canterbury Tales*.

If a man could afford it, keeping a mistress was thought a reasonable way of spending money. Edward III's mistress, Alice Perrers, inherited from him the manor of Wendover, an annuity and a collection of jewels that had belonged to the queen.

Jane Shore, the mistress of Edward IV, did rather badly however. Richard III, Edward's successor, had her accused of witchcraft, with the result that she spent her last years a beggar on the streets of London.

Dual morality condemned adultery and fornication in general, and held them to be more serious for women than for men — more because it was an insult to the man's honour than because it was morally reprehensible. In the eyes of the Church, even married sex was something to be tolerated only as a necessary evil. The only acceptable position was face-to-face, with the man on top, and the only days on which it was acceptable were those Mondays, Tuesdays and Thursdays which were not holy days or fasts. The worst day of all was Sunday.

John of Gaunt's daughter Elizabeth was destined to marry the Earl of Pembroke, one of the richest and most powerful men in England, until she was impregnated by the comparatively poor and lowly John Holland, to whom she had to be married in great haste.

Dress and make-up also came in for comment in pastoral books which posed such questions as to whether women had used monstrous apparel on their heads, or juiced (i.e. used make-up) with unguent or colour in order to appear redder or whiter to men. These were matters for censure.

In late medieval England, prostitution was regarded as something that could be entered into for a period when financial requirements made it attractive, with a return to respectable society possible, given the appropriate penance. In the Mediterranean on the other hand, the occupation was usually a one-way journey down the social ladder, and courtesans were kept apart in regulated brothels.

The Church was all in favour of saving 'fallen women,' and one fourteenth century nunnery at Montpellier in France was entirely composed of repentant or retired prostitutes – the Order of the Repentant Sisters of St Catherine. Religious demands upon such nuns were not onerous – a few 'Hail Marys' and 'Our Fathers' usually sufficed, with confession once a month.

So that prostitutes could be recognized, thus avoiding unnecessary embarassment, it was decreed in 1353 that they should not be allowed to wear hoods without stripes, furs or lined garments in London. They were also confined to 'red light' districts, such as Cock Lane in London (see also p. 118). This was not, of course, totally successful, and 'misguyded and idil women' and 'strumpettes' frequently could be found in 'respectable' taverns. One such was Dulcia de Gravesend, who plied her trade in 1266 in London.

A noblewoman's dress from c.1350 (Joan Nunn)

Some prostitutes used to rob clients when they were drunk. In 1263, Richard Vlet was robbed in this way, but was sufficiently sober to pull a knife and kill one of the 'strumpettes,' Beatrice de Wynton.

Children

Children did not have a happy lot in the Middle Ages. Infant mortality was extremely high, and accordingly parents tried not to become too attached to them. In particular, there is evidence of mothers being cold towards their daughters.

John and Margaret Paston named both their first two sons John, in the hope that one would survive so that a John Paston could inherit the estate.

Perinatal deaths were often attributed to 'overlaying' – the accidental suffocation of babies in bed with their parents.

Fathers were responsible for discipline, and were instructed to treat their children harshly in order to instil in them a proper sense of humility. In the upper echelons of society children were often sent away to fosterage in another family, so that they would not become spoiled and could learn useful skills. It was thus that pages were trained. Even amongst peasant society children were sometimes sent away due to the parents being unable to feed them.

On some occasions childrens' growth was deliberately stunted to produce a dwarf who could be sold for a good price as a court performer. A diet of knot-grass, dwarf-elder and daisies was considered good for this. The life of a court dwarf however was not a bad one.

Late 15c cradle, traditionally but erroneously believed to be that of Henry V (Jenny Laing)

2 · Castles

IN 1066, WILLIAM OF NORMANDY brought a prefabricated wooden donjon or fortress to England to establish at Hastings, and subsequently grossly accelerated the already existing trend towards fortified structures.

Castles, in particular stone crenellated examples, epitomize the vigour and variety of the medieval period. Some, such as Dover Castle which was built by the Normans, are still occupied by garrisons: others, such as Ewloe Castle, Wales, are romantic ruins. The latter, in its singularly picturesque sylvan setting, was unsuccessful, presumably due to having been built in a hollow surrounded by useful enemy vantage points.

In their many forms however, castles are testimony to the long period in British history when warfare on varying scales was a way of life. Virtually no area lacks a castle: estimates suggest that there are 1,700 in England and Wales, and that around AD1200 there were some 350 in active use. In Scotland the figures are comparable — around 1,000 (including tower houses of the sixteenth and seventeenth centuries). Estimates for Europe come to a massive 75,000–100,000 structures.

The Golden Age of castle-building extended from the eleventh to the fifteenth century, reaching a peak in the late thirteenth and early fourteenth, especially under Edward I. Although castles continued to be built into the sixteenth and seventeenth centuries, they started to go into terminal decline from the later fourteenth century onwards. A major factor in their demise was the invention and use of firearms. The Renaissance was also instrumental in separating military from domestic architecture because a more refined taste in interior comforts led noble families increasingly to prefer stately homes to cold draughty towers.

Castles were essentially private fortified residences, with battlements, that is, put up with a 'licence to crenellate' — a mark of status of an important noble family. Some heavily fortified manor houses, such as Tretower Court, Brecon, or Boothby Pagnell, Lincolnshire, were not strictly speaking castles, while others, such as Stokesay, Shropshire, are classified as castles, despite their domestic appearance.

The element of domestic occupation distinguished the medieval castle from other forms of fortification both before and since.

The Origins of Castle Architecture

Although the Normans were undoubtedly the most prolific castle builders in Britain, the origins of castles are hotly debated since

Ewloe, Clwyd. Early 13c native Welsh castle (Lloyd Laing)

there is evidence from Europe and Britain for castle-like structures being built before the Conquest. The development of castle architecture began in response to the feudal lords' need for residences which could be defended against rivals. The castle was both the stronghold from which the lord kept control of his lands and the symbol of the lordship itself. Here the troops were mustered, and here taxes were paid.

In the eleventh century, castles were essentially temporary structures made of earth and timber, and after the Third Crusade (1189–92) they were sited more carefully either against cliffs, or on the summits of hills.

In Britain, they come in two types: ringworks and mottes.

Ringworks These are earthen mounds which supported a timber superstructure, sometimes combined with a bailey, or outer banked enclosure. A good example of a Norman ringwork was that excavated at Penmaen in Glamorgan, with a timber gateway and palisaded bank enclosing timber buildings including a hall with a detached kitchen, later replaced by a crudely constructed hall with rounded corners.

Mottes There is some evidence that mottes were added to earlier ringworks, for example at Castle Neroche, Somerset, or Aldingham, Cumbria.

Examples of mottes are found throughout England and Wales with a dense concentration in the Marches (borders), reflecting the conflict between Normans and Welsh. In Scotland their spread coincided with the growth of Anglo-Norman influence in the twelfth century. Although they are concentrated in the Lowlands and in the fertile eastern strip, they are found as far north as Easter Ross. In Ireland they were thrown up by the Norman invaders in 1169, and are concentrated in the east.

These early structures are very different from those which the popular imagination typically fills with tapestries, ladies in tall headdresses and lords with greyhounds at their feet. As the excavator of the motte at Hen Domen has remarked,

Everything points to a life of great simplicity, shorn of extraneous trappings or ornament. The bailey is at all times overcrowded with buildings, but only two have any signs of heating ... The impression one gets is of a life of great hardiness, lived mainly out of doors, except in the worst weather and at night – not unlike all-year-round camping (Barker, P. 'Hen Domen Revisited', in Kenyon, J. & Avent, R. *Castles in Wales and the Marches*, Cardiff, 1987, 54)

The discovery here of two toe bones, a humerus, and half a cleft leather ankle boot is unusually graphic evidence of the perils of life.

In essence mottes comprised a mound and its quarry ditch, with a wooden bridge which led from the bailey. The motte itself would have been encircled with a palisade and crowned with a timber tower, though in Scotland the building material was possibly more often clay. The timber tower was probably clad, perhaps with wet hides or shields, and a sculptured capital at Westminster Abbey suggests that spears were thrust through holes giving it the appearance of a giant porcupine. Between the bailey and the motte there would have been a variety of buildings including a hall, chapel, stables, stores and smithy.

There is evidence that mottes displayed considerable variety and even fairly advanced technology in their design. While some, such as the one at Thetford, Norfolk, could attain a height of 24.5m (80 ft), many were much lower, and it is now appreciated that a main function of the mound was in many cases to stabilize the timber superstructure that was deeply embedded in the soil.

It has been calculated that the motte at Castle Neroche, Somerset, took around 13,780 working days to build, probably between four and six months.

The archaeologist Sir Arthur Evans (who is more famous for having discovered the Minoan civilization of Crete) built a motte with a summit 9m (30 ft) in diameter on Boars Hill, Oxford, in the 1930s. It took twenty men three years, using railway trucks and a crane.

At Abinger, Surrey, excavation showed that the motte was built before the tower, which was constructed with large corner posts embedded in it. On some sites, such as Ascot Doily in Oxfordshire and Castle Acre in Norfolk, the mounds were heaped up around the towers, which in these cases were made of stone.

Stone Castles

Stone castle building was most popular from the twelfth century onwards, when the keep (a tower-like structure containing a variety of facilities and the counterpart of the timber donjon), and curtain wall (the counterpart of timber palisades) made their appearance.

Keeps   There are only two eleventh-century stone castle keeps in England: the Tower of London and Colchester Castle, which stands on the foundations of Claudius' Roman temple and is still impressive despite the loss of its upper two floors.

The Tower of London is dominated by the Caen limestone keep, the White Tower, begun around 1078 with later concentric curtain walls around. It was so named because it was whitewashed in the time of Henry III, who had the downspouts lengthened to avoid unsightly stains.

Originally entered at first-floor level by means of an external wooden stairway or ladder (the original door is now a window), it followed the standard plan of having storerooms on the ground floor, the main public rooms on the first floor and the private apartments on the third.

The inner 'curtain' contains thirteen towers, of which the Bloody Tower is perhaps the most aptly named. Of the many executions and murders which took place in the Tower, one of the most famous examples involves the fate of two young princes. When Edward IV died aged forty in 1483, the victim, it was alleged, of his sexual excesses, his two young sons, Edward (proclaimed Edward V) and Richard, were left in the charge of Richard of Gloucester, later Richard III, who imprisoned them in the Tower. Whether he was in fact responsible for their subsequent deaths (and it has been long and hotly disputed), popular opinion has always blamed him.

In the early sixteenth century Sir Thomas More recorded that Richard III sent a message to the constable of the Tower telling him to give the keys to the Tower to one Sir James Tyrell for a solitary night. The two children were then smothered and buried at the foot of the

Bloody Tower. More said the bodies were later moved. In 1674 workmen demolishing a staircase outside the White Tower found a wooden chest containing the remains of two children. In 1933 the bones were examined medically, and reported as belonging to children of about ten and twelve years old. The elder child was suffering from a disease of the jaw, which might explain the 'depression' that Edward V was suffering from, as related by More.

The type of keep represented by the Tower of London continued to be built in later centuries, for example at Peveril, Derbyshire, or Kenilworth, Warwickshire, both of the twelfth century.

Keeps in the twelfth century and after   The construction of keeps continued during the twelfth century: that at Rochester was begun around 1127. The main building period, however, was the reign of Henry II (1154–89).

Peveril, Derbyshire. Square 12C keep, set within earlier curtain wall (Lloyd Laing)

LEFT: *Norwich Castle, early 12C hall keep, on heightened motte (Philip Dixon)*

There is a great diversity of details in the twelfth-century keeps or donjons. Many have buttresses, some have forebuildings to contain the entrance stair, and not a few have rooms contained inside the walls. Garderobes (latrines) are also found contrived in the thickness of the walls.

The earliest stone keeps in Scotland are Castle Sween, in Knapdale (Argyll), Cubbie Roo's Castle in Wyre (Orkney), which may be named after the Norse lord Kolbein Hruga and the Castle of Old Wick (Caithness).

Curtain walls   There are more surviving examples of eleventh-century stone curtain walls than keeps, though they too generally show signs of much later modifications. The outline of a curtain wall was dictated by geographical factors, but otherwise tended to be rectilinear and ideally was built on rock.

At Ludlow Castle in the Welsh Marches, the curtain was also furnished with a gateway and projecting rectangular towers. In the fullness of time the gateway was turned into a keep, and a number of other alterations were carried out, including the construction of an outer curtain wall enclosing an inner bailey.

At Peveril the twelfth-century keep (now entered at first-floor level by means of a modern replacement for the wooden medieval stair), stands within an eleventh-century curtain.

Shell keeps of the twelfth century   It was often impracticable to build a stone keep. Instead, a curtain wall was put up to circle the summit of the earlier mound, perhaps replacing a timber palisade. This produced an enclosed circular courtyard, in which stone or wooden buildings were constructed, often butted up against the curtain wall. Such castles are known as shell keeps.

In these cases the palisade along the summit of the bailey bank was similarly replaced by a curtain wall as can be seen at Windsor Castle, Carisbrooke in the Isle of Wight, Pickering in Yorkshire, and Launceston and Restormel in Cornwall.

In some cases the encircling wall of the shell keep was built not on top of the motte but around its base, for example at Berkeley Castle, Gloucestershire or Farnham Castle, Surrey.

Gatehouses   Gatehouses were elaborated in the thirteenth century, as a major element in defence. The curtain usually had a wall-walk and was flanked with towers which projected forwards to give flanking cover. The towers could be sealed off, so that if attackers gained possession of one section, they could not necessarily continue to the next without capturing the tower.

Edward I in Wales and Scotland

Thirteenth century innovations can be seen at their best in the castles built by Edward I in Wales. Edward's reign (1272–1307) marks the apogee of early medieval England. A contemporary judged him 'the best lance in the world'.

Edward's military campaigns were highly successful. In 1277 Llewellyn ap Gruffydd was forced to swear fealty to him, to pay an indemnity, and to surrender to Edward some parts of North Wales. Further resistance ended in Wales being given over to Edward's son (later to be Edward II) who was made the first Prince of Wales. Fine examples of castles of this period are to be found at Conway and Caernarfon.

Due to the very detailed records kept, a vivid picture of the organization of castle building can be built up from Edward I's North Welsh castles. We learn for example that Master James of St George (Edward's inspired architect) was awarded in 1284 the sum of three shillings a day for life (a huge sum at that time), along with half that again for his wife, Ambrosia. The building of Beaumaris required 400 masons, 2,000 labourers, and 30 smiths and carpenters, and records show that the Keepers of the See of Winchester were ordered to bring 1,000 quarters of wheat, 600 quarters of oats and 200 quarters of barley to Chester.

Stone was often brought substantial distances – that used at Harlech for example came partly from a source 11km (7 miles) to the south. Timber came from the Mersey estuary, lead from Shropshire and the Mendips. The cost of such a programme was enormous, and in six months at Beaumaris £6,500 was issued, necessitating the opening of a new mint at Chester.

Edward's campaigns in Scotland were less successful. A Scottish succession dispute led to one claimant, John Baliol, swearing fealty to Edward and being put in place as a puppet king (known to the Scots as Toom Tabbard, 'Empty Gown'). The Scottish nobles tried to restrict John Baliol's powers by negotiating for his son to marry a niece

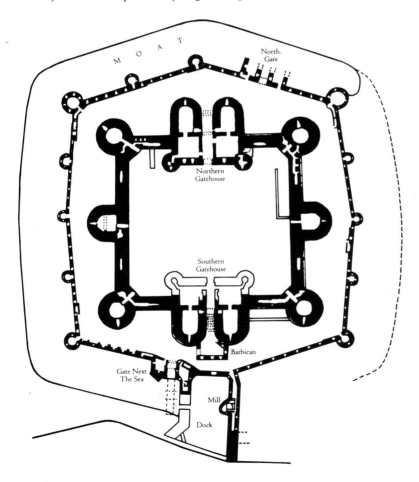

Plan of Beaumaris Castle, Anglesey, an Edwardian curtain wall castle.

of the King of France. As a result, war broke out, with Edward being victorious in a brief campaign in 1296–7.

In Scotland, Master James of St George usually constructed 'peels' – essentially ditched palisades, such as are known from Linlithgow (later used as the site for a fine palace) and Lochmaben, Dumfries.

At Kildrummy in Aberdeenshire however the existing curtain-wall stone castle, with its fine round towers, was further defended by a magnificent gatehouse which was the work probably of Master James of St George. The original castle, which has four drum towers, a hall and Gothic chapel, seems to have been inspired by the now destroyed French Château de Coucy. The Scottish King at the time, Alexander II, was married to Marie de Coucy, whose father built the French castle.

Siege Tactics

Many anti-siege tactics were probably quite unnecessary, except as part of psychological warfare, since very small garrisons could successfully defend substantial castles.

In the time of Henry II, Crowmarsh in Oxfordshire was successfully held by 160 men, and in 1216, Odiham in Hampshire was held for a week by three knights and two sergeants.

Pembroke castle had a standing garrison of two mounted men and ten foot soldiers in 1252. In 1319 Warksworth in Northumberland had twelve men-at-arms, despite a serious threat from the Scots to its north. Very few castles actually seem to have been subjected to extensive siege.

In addition to simple betrayal, the major problems to be faced were running out of food, water, or ammunition. A well was usually an essential in case of siege. Disease was a danger to a trapped population, and one useful attacking trick was to catapult filth or even animal corpses into castles, to encourage the spread of illnesses.

Failing good geographical conditions, the curtain wall could be protected by a wet moat, which prevented attackers from bringing siege engines up to its base. The problem with a moat however that it could be drained and filled in by attackers. In addition, the adjacent damp made the ground unstable and liable to subside. Therefore walls had to be thick (to withstand damp, and/or battering rams and, eventually, artillery), and high (to inhibit the projection of missiles over the top or scaling with ladders – a form of attack which was known as enfilading).

To further impede siege engines and sapping (see opposite), walls were often given a wide, splayed base (glacis), off which heavy stones could also be bounced on the attackers by the defenders on the wall-walks. The wall-walk could be carried out on corbels so that it extended over the heads of the attackers beneath – a type of extension known as a machicolation. Alternatively, a projecting timber wall-walk could be constructed. This has usually vanished, but the putlog holes for it are apparent in a number of castles, for example Threave, Kirkcudbright or Rothesay, on the Isle of Bute.

The top of the walls were crenellated, with alternating openings through which arrows or missiles could be projected, and raised

ABOVE AND OPPOSITE: *Siege engines – a mangon and a trebuchet* (Jenny Laing)

sections of parapet behind which archers could reload. Walls could also be made more impregnable with bastions.

Gates were defended by what is often erroneously termed a drawbridge. Rather than being 'drawn' up, bridges were more often of the counterweight type, with a pivot near the back like a see-saw, and heavy weights which sank back into a counterweight pit causing the bridge to close unless it was fastened with bolts.

The gatehouse itself was entered through a portcullis — a wooden grille with iron cladding that was lowered by chains attached to winches in the room above the passage way. The passage was flanked by guard chambers, with arrow slits, and in the room above there were sometimes holes in the floor through which projectiles could be aimed at those successful enough to attain the passage way.

Sometimes a barbican, or protective tower, was constructed to force the attackers into an enclosed section in which they could be picked off by defenders. Ideally, this involved making the attackers present their right (undefended) side to the defenders, which is why the circular staircases in most towers spiralled clockwise.

Castles were often furnished with a postern — a small 'back door' usually in an inconspicuous situation difficult of access, which allowed escape if the the besiegers were victorious.

A common tactic of besiegers was to erect two lines of palisading round the castle (the inner was the contravallation, the outer the circumvallation) representing their camp and also serving to trap escapers.

Essential weaknesses of rectangular towers were the corners, which could be 'sapped' (undermined), to cause part of the tower to collapse. To combat this, towers with curved wall-faces were introduced and became an almost universal feature of thirteenth-century castle architecture.

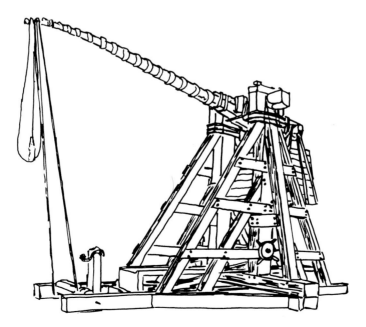

The construction of circular keeps began around 1200, and was heralded at Pembroke which was built for the English expedition to Ireland.

The design was taken up by the Welsh princes of North Wales, who having first built Anglo-Norman style rectangular keeps, such as Dolwydellan, Gwynedd, built around 1170, adopted the circular plan for Dolbadarn in the same area early in the thirteenth century.

A variant was the D-shaped keep. This was a rare experiment which can be seen at the native Welsh castle at Ewloe in Clwyd, datable to around 1210.

Besieging Tactics

One of the more popular tactics was sapping, a process which necessitated lighting fires in a tunnel under the wall. King John took Rochester Castle, Kent, by sapping in 1214, and Bedford Castle was taken in the same way in 1224. However, this method, and that of scaling the walls by ladders, were impossible until moats had been filled in. This was done under cover of a movable shed, called a 'cat' or 'sow', which had a rawhide roof to protect those filling the moat from fire from above.

The first siege engine was the mangon, or mangonel. This depended on the tension produced by twisting a skein of hairs and gut into which the end of an arm was slotted. At the opposite end was a cup which was loaded with a boulder, perhaps of about 2cwt (102kg/224 lb), which was hauled down and held by a trigger mechanism. On release, the arm flew up against a cross frame and the impact propelled the stone.

When Dunbar castle, East Lothian, was besieged in 1328, mangonels and a sow were both used by the attackers.

The Countess of Dunbar, 'Black Agnes', ordered a girl with a towel to wipe away the dust created by stones from the mangonels on the battlements, and smashed the sow brought up by the assailant, by catapulting stones from the battlements with the florid rhetoric: 'Montague, I sall gar thy sow farrow against her will'.

The counterweight principle was successfully employed in the trebuchet, which was developed by the French in the twelfth century, not becoming popular until the thirteenth century. It had a pivot, one end of which was weighted, the other attached to a sling. A bridle attached to the sling from the arm controlled the trajectory. The arm was winched down with a windlass, and held again by a trigger mechanism. It went by a number of names in medieval literature – onager, scorpion, petary, perrier and catapult, for example.

The arblast or espringale was the descendant of the Roman ballista and was essentially a giant cross-bow on a carriage, which propelled javelins.

Another useful item in the besiegers' equipment was the 'beffroi' or belfry, a wooden tower on wheels which could be trundled up to the walls, and which in theory was constructed tall enough for a bridge to be lowered at the top over the wall-walk.

Experiments were carried out at White Castle, Monmouth, to test the efficacy of long bows in castle warfare. It was demonstrated by shooting arrows through arrow slits that it was possible to provide adequate flanking cover of all the fields at the base of the wall with only one dead zone. It was also demonstrated however that besiegers could enjoy a reasonable measure of success in shooting arrows through arrowslits from the outside of the castle.

An analysis has also been made of the defensive capabilities of Framlingham Castle, Suffolk, where fifty-six men formed the garrison in 1216. It was calculated that every stretch of the southern front of the castle could be covered by arrows when the garrison was at full strength. The oval circuit had thirteen square towers, open at the back and with removable floors, which allowed four men per tower and length of wall for its defence.

Livery and Maintenance and Bastard Feudalism

In the later Middle Ages there was something of a return to older traditions of castle building, for practical considerations usually relating to dwindling numbers of soldiers available for a garrison.

In the time of Henry I scutage was introduced, by which a vassal could pay for every shield (scutum), or soldier, he was due to put in the field, instead of the forty days military service levy. Such a financial arrangement between king and vassal became known as bastard feudalism. Normally the scutage was two marks (£1.75 in modern terms), which was then used to pay mercenaries who were better trained and prepared to fight for long periods. Henry II employed mercenaries in his foreign wars, and under John and Henry III it became very common – the Magna Carta has a clause stipulating that foreign men-at-arms and crossbowmen should be banished.

Soldiers of fortune had the disconcerting habit of defecting to any enemy who was prepared to pay more: nevertheless, their use increased during the later fourteenth century when the French wars were going badly.

Such risks are reflected in later castle design where the lord increasingly had to look to his own defence and his private quarters had to be able to be sealed off and quite separate from those of his retainers. To this end the gatehouse was frequently seen as a suitable subject for development, so that it became in effect a gatehouse keep.

Edward I employed the idea of the gatehouse keep in some of his Welsh castles. At Harlech, for instance, the constable made his private quarters in the fortified gatehouse. Access to the first floor was only possible by means of a stair from the inside of the courtyard, so that if the lower part of the gatehouse with its entrance was captured, the upper part could still be defended.

Later still, castles not unlike the keeps of the twelfth century were built. Sometimes these stood alone, sometimes within a curtain-wall system of defence. Good examples are Ashby-de-la-Zouche in Leicestershire, Nunney in Somerset, Tattershall in Lincolnshire and Raglan in Monmouth.

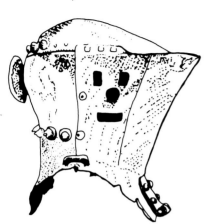

Tilting helmet, found in Melbury Sampford church, Dorset (Lloyd Laing)

Arms and Armour

The armour of the Norman conquerors appears in the Bayeux Tapestry – they wore chain hauberks which reached below their knees, and sometimes mail stockings. As the mailcoat was not totally effective against spears and arrows, a padded tunic was worn underneath. Norman helmets were conical caps with a protective nose guard.

Chain mail, with interlinked rings, remained the most important type of armour during the succeeding period down to the later fourteenth century, though it became shorter, not going below the knees, and a mail hood was employed to protect the head, under which was a padded cap. The twelfth century saw the introduction of the great helm, which was cylindrical with eye slits and was worn in battle. Ordinary footsoldiers wore a broad-brimmed metal helmet called a kettle hat. From the end of the thirteenth century another type of helmet was favoured – the basinet – which fitted the head closely and had a hinged vizor. In the fourteenth century the vizor had a long point, and helmets with this were known as 'pig-faced basinets'.

Armour made of metal plates made its appearance in the later thirteenth century. Initially these plates were added to chain mail, on vulnerable points, but in due course the full suit of armour was developed. This came into its own in the fifteenth century, when the armour used in Britain mostly came from the Continent, notably Italy and Germany. Not only knights but their horses were protected in this way. In the fourteenth century horse armour was restricted, but in the fifteenth the knight's charger had a chafron or chamfrein to protect its face, a neck guard (crinet), a breastplate (petral), flank plates (flanchards) and a hindquarters plate (crupper).

Longbows were important in warfare from the twelfth century, and crossbows, which had first been used in Roman times (and which are known in Dark Age Scotland) were particularly common in the later Middle Ages, when armour-piercing bodkin points were favoured, as well as bullet-shaped arrowheads for the same purpose. Cannon were first used in England in the fourteenth century. One appears in a manuscript of 1326, and evidence suggests that they were first used in campaign at Crécy in 1346. Hand-guns were simply miniature cannon, a fifteenth-century example of which has been found at Castle Rising, Norfolk.

Axes were used in battle in the Norman period, and the medieval period as a whole saw the use of maces, spears, lances, daggers and of course swords. Quillon daggers were like miniature swords, with projecting guards for the hand, while rondel daggers had a guard and pommel of flat discs. The ballock dagger had two projecting lobes at the base of the hilt.

Ballock or kidney dagger, with wooden hilt. Late 14th or early 15th century, Caerlaverock Castle, wet moat (Historic Scotland)

Norman swords were mostly derived from the types of the Viking period, but later swords were larger with longer quillons, and typically, in the thirteenth century, had round pommels. With the development of plate armour came the hand-and-a-half sword or bastard sword, which had longer grips so the weapon could be used with two hands if the occasion arose.

Firing positions   Up until the late fourteenth century, arrow slits had sufficed for the launching of firepower. However, with the introduction of cannon, slits were gradually replaced by gun loops. These first appear at the end of the fourteenth century, and began by having profiles not unlike arrow slits, with a round opening at the bottom like an inverted keyhole.

They were first used in a town gate, Canterbury Westgate, in 1380. In 1386 Bodiam Castle, Sussex, was built entirely for coastal defence, with inverted keyhole gunloops in its gatehouse.

Castle Embellishments

Increasingly, castles became homes rather than elements in a defensive scheme. As the Wars of the Roses came to a end in the final years of the Middle Ages, castles started to use features of undefended architecture, such as thinner walls, larger windows, ornamental details and greater comfort.

At Kenilworth, Warwickshire, for example, John of Gaunt built a hall in the late fourteenth century with superb traceried windows, in the shadow of the grim twelfth-century keep. Brick was increasingly employed, and can be seen, for example, at Herstmonceaux, Sussex, or Tattershall, Lincolnshire, and the military features such as gun loops or arrow slits start to look more ornamental than functional.

Moated Manors

As noted at the beginning of this chapter, not all fortified residences in medieval Britain were castles. Moated sites are even more numerous than castles, with over five thousand recorded in England and Wales. They are particularly found on the claylands, with concentrations in Essex, Suffolk, Yorkshire and Lincolnshire.

Moated sites are areas, usually rectilinear (though they can be almost any shape including round or D-shaped), bounded by a ditch which was normally filled with water. In most cases, a house (usually a manor) and ancillary buildings were contained within this enclosure, though there were also double moated sites where one moat may have been used to enclose a garden or orchard. The buildings constructed on moated sites tended to be of wood or of cob walling, though stonework is sometimes encountered.

There is little evidence for moated sites before the thirteenth century, and they may well have been status symbols used by lesser knights and freemen to proclaim their social position. Many also seem to reflect the opening up of forest lands. The construction of moated sites how-

Hilt of hand-and-a-half sword, River Thames, Sion Reach, 2nd quarter of fifteenth century (Lloyd Laing)

ever declined from the second quarter of the fourteenth century, and after 1500 moated sites, like castles, were progressively abandoned in favour of greater comfort.

Later Scottish Castles

In Scotland castles followed a somewhat divergent pattern of development from that in England. During the early fourteenth century few actual castles were built due to the Wars of Independence. Instead the tower house – essentially a keep – emerged as the dominant type of castle. It persisted until the seventeenth century.

A good fourteenth century example of such a tower house can be seen at Loch Leven, where Mary Queen of Scots was imprisoned before being taken south to face her doom in England.

Scottish architects were highly inventive in the building of tower houses. They contrived complexes of chambers inside the walls, which grew ever thicker, and access between floors was achieved by means of a single spiral staircase.

By the fifteenth century tower houses had acquired some of the luxuries of life, such as the occasional fireplace and built-in cupboard, but in the interval it was decided to add a wing to provide domestic accommodation. This is known as a jam, and produced what is termed the L-plan.

The door to the tower was protected in the angle between the main block and the jam, and could be given flanking fire from two sides. A good example of this type of castle can be seen at Craigmillar, just outside Edinburgh.

Scotland did not however escape the problem of defecting garrisons, and in addition to the tower houses can be seen castles that were the outcome of bastard feudalism, where the lord had to defend himself against the possible rebellion of his garrison. The best example is Tantallon, East Lothian, where a curtain wall cuts off a promontory defended by a cliff. Within the enclosed area are two halls, one above the other, the lower for the garrison, the upper for the laird.

The earliest artillery fortification in Britain can be seen in Scotland, at Ravenscraig, Fife, built by James I and starting around 1460 as part of a scheme for coastal defence.

Tournaments and The Joust

Warfare was not without its offshoot entertainments, in the form of ritualized battles, known as tournaments, in inspiring literature and music and, especially, the concept of chivalry that was so pervasive at the time. Tournaments seem to have been invented in the eleventh century, by Geofroy de Preuilly. They were particularly a feature of French courtly life, and were far less popular in England, except in the time of Edward III.

In essence, a tournament was a battle in which prisoners were taken, and, although deaths could occur, they were chiefly symbolic enactments of the type of events that were taking place in reality. The career

OPPOSITE ABOVE: *Stokesay, Shropshire, a fortified manor house of the 12th and 13th centuries in a moated walled enclosure with 16c gatehouse (Philip Dixon)*

OPPOSITE BELOW: *Stokesay, interior of great hall (Philip Dixon)*

of Richard I ('The Lionheart', 1189–99), warrior and poet, exemplifies the way of life. He spent only about six months of his reign in England, the rest of his time being taken up with a crusade and his campaigns against the encroachment of the French King Philip Augustus on English territory in France during which he finally died, besieging Chalus. On his return journey from the crusade he had been captured, handed over to the Emperor Henry VI, and released only when a huge ransom was paid.

Hardly surprisingly, Richard posthumously became the subject of many romances. For instance, according to later French tradition the poet Blondel de Nesle wandered through Austria in an attempt to find the imprisoned King. Outside the walls of a particular castle he sang half a song which he and the King had composed jointly. Richard then continued singing, proving his identity and whereabouts.

The eldest son of Henry II took up tournaments as a pastime, and it is notable that only the very rich could afford to maintain teams of knights, or the payments of huge ransoms that became due to the captors. Indeed, younger sons could and did find fortunes this way. In the case of Henry II's heir, he was able to marry the heiress of Richard de Clare, which brought him much of South Wales, the castles of Pembroke and Chepstow, the honour of Crendon and the kingdom of Leinster.

The joust was a small-scale tournament which was increasingly popular from the fourteenth century. It was a one-to-one combat with any of a variety of weapons, carried out on horseback or on foot, from which the combatants usually escaped with not much worse than serious bruises. Jousts were also indulged in as the opening of a tournament, and up-market events had tourneys interspersed with jousts and feasts, over several days.

As time went on the tournaments became increasingly entertainments rather than practice wars, with music, dancing, and betting. A shocked monastic chronicler in 1348 recorded how forty 'wanton' women dressed as men in multi-coloured garments paraded through the lists on chargers and palfreys. They then 'forgot' their marriage vows, and indulged in lewd behaviour.

The Black Prince's crested iron helm (John Ferguson)

Heraldry

Heraldry was a by-product of feudalism and chivalry, as its primary function was to enable particular knights to be recognized immediately on the field. The coat of arms became of particular importance after about 1180, when the closed helmet meant that the face of the knight could not be seen. Family badges are of considerable antiquity – they appear on coins struck in Athens in the sixth century BC for example. However, the blazon (the name originally was given to the shield, then to the device upon it) seems to have been developed first in France before soon spreading to England. Its adoption was further spread by the increased use of seals and in inherited surnames.

Initially, the heraldic devices were displayed on shields and banners, but as shields were reduced in size in the thirteenth century, the de-

14c tournament pavilion

Jousting knights from the *Manessa Codex*

Arms of
William the Marshall

Lance heads

The English court rolls present a catalogue of crime, misdemeanour and punishment in the countryside which is mostly predictable — trespass of cattle, neglect of land or buildings, defiling of common springs or digging of clay pits in the public roads.

'Common thieves of poultry' are often mentioned, as are tenants who stole firewood from the hedges, moved boundary stones or took such things as a stranded porpoise or a find of wild honey.

Land Management

The Celts and Romans had enclosed their fields, in much the same way as is done today, and the countryside was interspersed with small settlements which were to various degrees connected to the network of towns. During the Middle Ages however, until the enclosures (which began around 1300) the agrarian landscape comprised open fields approached by tracks which ran around. The winding English lanes can nowadays often be seen to traverse such old field systems rather than going directly from A to B.

Since few people were either permitted to, or needed to travel far, this system would have worked adequately — road building, for example, was not a feature of the medieval period.

The medieval rural landscape was very different from that which prevails today and in general, all that remains are the bumps and hollows of cultivation and the pattern of lanes sometimes visible within larger fields.

The unfenced fields were cultivated in terms of a unit called a land. This was a strip of about one third of an acre (about 7×180m on average — $7\frac{1}{2} \times 200$ yds). Each was ploughed clockwise, forming a ridge in the middle about 0.3m (1 ft) above the lowest level, and with furrows on either side. This is the ridge-and-furrow familiar to all students of the medieval landscape. The ridging helped drainage. Groups of ridges usually have a twist at the end, creating a reversed S shape, distinguishing them from the straight nineteenth-century steam plough ridges. The process of ploughing left a small amount of earth deposited at the end of the ridge where the plough was turned, and with time this formed a bank termed a head or butt.

Groups of lands lying in the same direction were called furlongs. Where groups of furlongs were running at angles to one another two heads were formed, and these were often allowed to grass over to become pathways called balks. Triangular areas filling in odd areas were termed gores. Furlongs were grouped together into fields, and villages farmed two, later three fields in crop rotation.

Meadows were similarly divided up into strips, but since they were not ploughed they have left no trace.

Open field farming involves a number of important elements: subdivided fields, common pasture or fallow, common waste and a manorial court to control the system. In the past historians have argued that this was the outcome of agricultural necessity in the twelfth or thirteenth century, but there is growing evidence that it was well established by the twelfth.

ABOVE: *Ploughing, Luttrell Psalter, c.1340. Additional MS 42130, f. 181 (British Library)*

LEFT: *Ridge and Furrow. Remains of medieval cultivation at Heronbridge, Cheshire (Jenny Laing)*

There has been considerable debate among archaeologists about when and where open-field farming and ridge-and-furrow cultivation originated. Traces were found under the motte at Hen Domen, Montgomery, and thus were pre-Conquest, and at Bentley Grange, in Yorkshire, mining tips of the twelfth century overlay it.

Estate maps are particularly useful in studying early ridge-and-furrow since they show who held which strips in particular fields. The accompanying record books listing the holdings are called terriers. The most useful of these are parish books, called field books or town books. Field books are known from the fourteenth century.

Late Saxon charters use terms which relate to open-field farming — charters of 962 and around 977 at Hendred and Kingston in Oxfordshire show that a mixed strip system was in operation there. There is also some evidence that the original layout involved much larger fields, in which the strips were later subdivided.

The allocation of strips to tenants was a matter for the manorial court rolls, and manorial accounts provide information about work done, manuring etc. Such records go back to the thirteenth century. The amount of land allocated to each peasant was known as a bovate or virgate, and could vary from 17 to 40 acres (7–16 hectares). Between forty and eighty strips were allocated to each farmer in the various fields, and the allocation had to allow for fallow. Similarly, there was strict regulation about the number of animals that could be kept.

67

Domesticated animals Archaeological evidence from excavated villages suggests small numbers of animals. At Wythemail (a deserted medieval village in Northamptonshire) a single farm enclosure produced bones from five cattle and five sheep. The latter were mature animals, killed after their lives as effective wool producers were over. At Wharram Percy, Yorkshire, a highland site, sheep outnumbered cattle (60 per cent sheep, 30 per cent oxen, 8 per cent pig and 2 per cent deer), a proportional spread found on other sites. Here killing seems to have been done after two years, in contrast to the situation at Wythemail.

Laxton – a 'modern' medieval village The only place in England where open-field farming is still carried on is Laxton in Nottinghamshire, though the strip system has been modified to suit modern machinery.

Laxton is a remarkable time-capsule of medieval village life which deliberately made a decision to remain in the traditional system at the time of the sweeping reforms made in Land Law in 1925. Although the village houses have been rebuilt in later centuries, the village plan is probably much as it was in the Middle Ages, and is focused on a twelfth- and thirteenth-century church and a fine motte.

Land in Laxton is divided between three open fields, the West, South and Mill Fields, and a few enclosed areas. There are two commons. The open fields are smaller than they once were, but the division of land has not radically changed for at least seven centuries.

The Mill Field is first mentioned in 1189, though part of it at least was probably farmed earlier. The fields were worked on a three-field rotation, with one field left fallow. This system was modified in 1967 as the number of animals in the village had diminished, and a forage crop grown in the fallow field.

Laxton still operates its manorial court, which meets in the Dovecote Inn in late November or early December. It appoints a jury of twelve to inspect the fallow field, and to make sure that the farmers have ploughed only their share and have not encroached on neighbouring strips.

The roadways are inspected and marked with stakes, and after lunch at the inn there is a hearing of farming offences committed. A week later the inn is the setting for the Court Leet, which discusses all the communal business.

There was some enclosure at Laxton in the earlier eighteenth century, and again in the earlier twentieth. Since 1981 the Crown Estate Commissioners have been the lords of the manor.

Innovations in farming The Middle Ages saw the first agrarian revolution, when important developments were made in farming techniques and patterns of rural life were established. These innovations mainly belong to the period prior to the fourteenth century and two of the knock-on effects were a basic change in diet, and the evolution of the complex pattern of marriage and inheritance customs, devised to protect land interests (see p. 31). Both these developments were to last for centuries.

One of the chief rural developments during the Middle Ages was the cultivation of leguminosi (especially peas), which was concentrated in east and south-east England and the east Midlands. Fields left fallow could be cropped and their fertility improved.

There was growing understanding of different forms of soil improvers, and marl, sand, sea-weed and lime were all employed. Square shaped ponds that represent flooded medieval marl pits are a feature of many parts of the countryside today.

The development of crop rotation was another innovation, with a change-over from the two-field to three-field system which became increasingly common after 1300.

A further novelty, found in the east Midlands and eastern England, was the use of small horses to pull the plough, instead of traditional oxen. This doubled the amount of land that could be ploughed in a given time.

Woodland and forest management   For many years it was believed that at the time of the Norman Conquest much of Britain was covered with woodland, which was gradually encroached upon by medieval farmers. Archaeology has now demonstrated that land was gradually opened up from the forest over a very long period from the fourth millennium BC onwards. By late Saxon times only about 15 per cent of England was woodland, though much larger areas of Scotland were still fairly densely covered with trees. Many villages were as much as a day's journey from a substantial area of woodland and forests covered only about 3 per cent of England.

Woods and forests however played an important role in the economy and society of medieval England, and woodland management was well developed. Unlike some more recent societies, that of the Middle Ages understood that natural resources had to be maintained by controlled exploitation and replacement. Coppicing was fully comprehended, with cycles ranging from four to twenty-eight years.

The kings were cognisant with conservation, and orders were passed that trees should be left standing if felling would damage the forest. Woodlands and forests were located in areas such as steep hills or bad soil where other crops could not flourish.

In addition to woods, forests were kept for royal deer hunting, and were subject to their own laws. They were not solid areas of trees, but contained farmland, villages and private parks.

Village Plans

The majority of medieval village houses were probably flimsy, and, with the passage of time have been replaced, often in brick or stone during the nineteenth century. However, a number of villages retain emotive atmospheres, even though the buildings are of more recent date, because of their medieval origins. A much photographed example is Finchingfield in Essex.

While there is no such thing as a truly 'typical' medieval village, generally speaking they had a main street or a green, around which the

*Peasant house reconstructed at Singleton
Open Air Museum, Sussex
(Acorn Media/Slide Centre Ltd)*

tofts and crofts of the villagers were disposed in a fairly regular manner.

A toft was a rectangular enclosure with a house and outbuildings. Behind it lay the croft, which was a long enclosure usually running back to a boundary bank that served to delimit the village.

The crofts were enclosed, and the interior of the toft was often slightly raised above the surrounding area, either due to deliberate planning, or from the accumulation of debris. The village also usually had a manor house, within its own moat, and a church (see chapters 2 and 4).

Where village houses do survive they are normally of the fifteenth century, and comprise one-storey cruck-houses constructed with pairs of curved timbers (traditionally made from the trunk and lowest branch of an oak), the commonest type of which had one bay. Good examples of cruck buildings can be seen at Weobley, Hereford.

In the fifteeenth century the rise of more prosperous yeoman farmers led to the building of more sumptuous dwellings, inspired by town houses. They varied from two to six rooms in size, with a hall as the main feature, and were frequently detached from their farm buildings.

With the exception of such late medieval yeoman's houses, most houses are known only from archaeological excavation, the majority of these from deserted villages (see p. 79).

There were three types of village house: the cot, the long-house and the farm. The cot, the most lowly village house, was usually rectangular and no more than 5m (5½ yds) wide and 10m (11 yds) long. Each had one, or sometimes two rooms.

Slightly more prosperous members of the village could aspire to long-houses. As the name suggests, these were narrow rectangular buildings, and were distinguished by having byre and domestic accommodation under the same roof alignment. This arrangement is highly cost-effective since the animals give off considerable heat.

A cross-passage in the long sides normally separated the dwelling from the byre which, in areas where arable farming predominated, was used for storage. Long-houses can be up to 30m (33 yds) long, but were no more than 5m (5½ yds) wide, to enable the roof to span the floor space. Usually there was a small room segmented off from the main dwelling area, for the master and mistress.

In the fourteenth century, farmhouses appeared as the homes of the richest peasants, who were able to afford the luxury of keeping animals in a separate byre. The house and byre were usually arranged around a yard at right angles to one another. It may have been that declining population meant the pressure on land was not as great — on some excavated sites single farms seem to have been built on top of the sites of several successive long-houses.

At Gomeldon in Wiltshire, house development can clearly be seen. On one plot a small twelfth-century long-house was replaced by two larger structures in the earlier thirteenth century, which were in turn replaced by a farm complex within the century. The farms may have been owned by those who had become rich enough to buy their freedom from their feudal lords.

Building materials   Until the thirteenth century, wood was the main building material, with substantial structural timbers infilled with panels of wattle-and-daub or sometimes of turf. Where turf walls were used, the inner faces were lined with wattle, for example at Hound Tor, Devon. As the thirteenth century progressed however stone replaced timber, and the new houses were either built entirely of stone or with a timber superstructure on top of low walls.

Floors were of beaten earth or clay, sometimes with cobbles for patches of heavy wear, though floorboards are also known. The floors were kept very clean with regular sweeping which often resulted in the inside of the house being lower than the ground outside.

Family members would have been warmed by a hearth without a chimney in the centre of the living space, though on occasion there was a wattle-and-daub canopy to direct smoke to the smoke-hole.

The roof was usually covered in turf, though slates were also used. Most houses were single-storeyed, but traces of a stair to an upper floor were found at Seacourt, Berks.

Lower Brockhampton House, Hereford & Worcs. Moated 14c manor house with later gatehouse (Philip Dixon)

Tithe Barns

A tithe (tenth) of villagers' produce was given to the Church, and where tithe barns survive they are an indication that the parish church had connections with a major monastery. They were often splendid buildings with fine timber-framed roofs and stone walling. At Great Coxwell in Oxfordshire a thirteenth-century barn connected with the Abbey of Beaulieu still exists.

An outstanding tithe barn at Peterborough, built in 1307, was

Great Coxwell, Oxfordshire, tithe barn of Beaulieu Abbey, first decade of 14th century (Philip Dixon)

RIGHT: *Interior, Great Coxwell (Philip Dixon)*

demolished at the end of the nineteenth century, since it stood on a plot of land desirable for 'development'. It was calculated that three houses could be built on the site, which was sold, barn and all, for £1100.

Diet

Diet, like farm produce, varied considerably from region to region. The medieval male peasant ate as much as five pounds of bread a day (about 60 rolls), which provided 5,000 calories and, due to the recipes which differed from modern bread, at least 200 grams of protein. Meat-eating was mostly found in the highland zone. Documentary evidence suggests that meat may also have played an important role in affluent lowland areas such as Huntingdonshire. In southern England bread was supplemented by dairy produce, herring, onions, leeks and garlic. In Cheshire oat cakes were preferred to bread. Oats were commonly grown in the highland zone, where they were the best crop for the soil conditions and where they were eaten as porage and increasingly needed for horses. The most popular vegetable was the cabbage, eaten by both rich and poor.

Large quantities of ale were consumed, probably often brewed by the wives of the poorer cottars. In the fifteenth century the famous Margery Kemp of King's Lynn was both a mystic and a brewer, although it is not recorded whether these two factors were related. Another fifteenth-century thinker (for other reasons considered a heretic), expressed the view that there was more good in a cask of ale than in the four Gospels.

A distinction was made between beer and ale from Anglo-Saxon times onwards, hops being added to beer to give it a bitter flavour and to make it keep longer. The late Saxon Graveney boat was filled with hops, though prior to this discovery the use of hops was attributed to the Dutch and dated to around 1400. Villagers also drank cider, depending on the region.

Vineyards are well documented and although some were cultivated before the Norman Conquest, many more were established after it. According to Domesday Book, Suffolk boasted four vineyards, and Essex ten. South Middlesex had seven vineyards, Kent three, Berkshire one, Wiltshire four. The clerks recording the information for Wilcot, Wilts, noted that it was a 'good vineyard', which, it has been pointed out, could only have been known if its products had been sampled by the commissioners. The peasantry did not drink wine.

The skeletons from the excavated, deserted village of Wharram Percy, Yorkshire, suggest a robust society, but rheumatic diseases were common, as were tooth decay and gall and bladder stones.

The Rural Economy – Career Openings

Although the basis of the rural economy was farming, the economy was fairly open, with trade playing a secondary role. Hunting supplemented the diet, and hunting arrowheads are common finds. Wolf hunting was not an unknown occupation. In the time of Henry VI, Robert Plumpton held wolf-hunt land in Sherwood Forest, while in the time of Edward III, Thomas Engaine held lands at Pitchley on condition he found dogs at his own expense for wolf and fox hunting.

Wolves seem to have died out in England in the time of Henry VII, but they survived in Scotland into the seventeenth century, the last wolf being killed at Bettyhill in Sutherland. There were wild boars in Savernake and in County Durham in the time of Henry VII, (though most boars had vanished by the late thirteenth century) and beavers were still to be found on the Teifi in South Wales when Giraldus Cambrensis was writing in the twelfth century, although along with the lynx and the bear they were extinct in England by the Norman Conquest.

Rabbits were introduced by the Normans, and were kept in artificially-created warrens, now known as pillow mounds.

Fish was often traded over considerable distances – cod bones were found at Wharram Percy in Yorkshire, some 30km (18½ miles) from the coast. At Bredwardine in Hereford scales from perch have been found in medieval pond silts. Documentary sources show that pike was the most popular delicacy, followed by eels, tench, bream, perch and roach.

Fishponds seem to have been essential features of most manors in southern England in the Middle Ages. Some of these were very ambitious, with complex earthworks and systems of sluices and dams. They took different forms – rectangular ponds fed by a stream or spring, pools dammed with stone or timber revetments, and hillslope ponds.

The village blacksmith is badly represented in the archaeological record, but horseshoes and spurs are fairly common finds, and 20 per cent of the bones found in the excavations at Wharram Percy were of horses. Coal seems to have travelled up to 200km (124 miles) from its source to quite remote villages.

Ironwork is not abundantly found on village sites, but occasional agricultural implements come to light. The spade was of wood, but iron shod, the shoe being shrunk on to the wood. They were used among other purposes for well digging, and one was found in a well in the deserted village at Lyveden, Lincs. Wooden spades are sometimes found – one came from a Norman pit at Pevensey, Sussex.

Ploughs are rarely represented in archaeological finds, as they were mostly of wood, but had additionally a coulter – a knife-blade for cutting a furrow slice in front of the plough – and a share, which covered the wooden end of the plough and turned the furrow started by the coulter.

Other agricultural implements include pruning hooks, hayforks, billhooks, axes, and sickles, as well as sheep shears that are little different from those still in use. Spuds were iron blades used to remove earth from implements.

Typical 14c peasant dress (Joan Nunn)

Sickles, Caerlaverock, Dumfriesshire
(Historic Scotland)

Three men mowing. A misericord from Worcester Cathedral, c.1379 (by permission of the Dean and Chapter of Worcester)

Each village had its own wind or watermill, and one long-house at Upton was given over to the fulling of cloth. Domesday Book documents 5,624 mills, presumably water-driven.

A common oven was sometimes found in English villages — in France, where it was more commonplace, it was called a *four banal* — the bread produced in it was considered inferior, hence the modern English word, 'banal'.

Spinning and weaving seem to have been done at home, to judge by finds of spindle whorls (for weighting the spindle) and loom weights.

Most excavated villages have produced some pottery, usually including fine glazed wares (chapter 9).

Names — People and Places

The wide variety of experience and rapidly changing society of rural Britain are reflected in the many personal and place names that originate from the medieval period.

One of the first changes the Normans made was in the place names. These changes came about partly through Domesday Book and partly through the deliberate renaming of settlements. The number of place-names totally replaced by the Normans however was not great, but they include Beaumont (Essex), which means 'beautiful hill' and was a dramatic replacement of Fulanpettae, a 'foul pit'!

It is to the Normans and their French successors that modern England owes the majority of French-derived place names. Wharram Percy in Yorkshire was held by William de Perci in 1177 and Huish Champflower, (Somerset) was the hide or household which was held in 1212, by Thomas de Chanflurs (after Champfleury in Normandy). Bere (burgh) Ferrers (Byrfferers in 1239) was held by William de Ferrers in 1242, and derives from one of the *ferrières* (smitheries) in Normandy. Tolleshunt D'Arcy derives its name from one Robert Darcy who got land there in 1441, the name coming from Arcy in Normandy.

Many French-derived place names were not transplanted from the Continent, but are simply descriptions. Belvoir (pronounced Beever) in Leicestershire means a 'beautiful view'. Grosmont (Monmouthshire) however, meaning 'big hill', is probably a direct implantation.

Even when the earlier Celtic and Saxon names remained, the spelling and the pronunciation was modified in time. *Th* for example, was replaced with *t*, as in Tarleton and the *Y* became *J* as in Jarrow. Through this sort of scribal change the name Searoburg eventually developed into Salisbury.

Although the language of trade and the court under the Normans, the Angevins and the Plantaganets was French, official documents were written in Latin. Thus from the medieval period come such place names as Chapel-en-le-Frith, and those which include words such as Magna, Parva or Cum.

Land-use can also be commemorated in field names. The majority of these derive from the later medieval or post-medieval period since the open field system was employed before this time, but some are relevant here. For example, a reminder that the countryside differed from today lies in field names such as Wolueacres (recorded in 1372 at Haughton), and Wlueshall (recorded in 1278 at Church Coppenhall, Cheshire and meaning wolf's nook).

A wide variety of animals feature in field names – from moles and hedgehogs to partridges – though many cannot be dated as early as the period under review. One such example however is Enedewong, recorded *c*.1200 at Flitcham in Norfolk, and referring to a duck's 'wong' (field). Several fields in the fourteenth century were named after hawks.

Service to the lord was required of lowly members of society, and one example is the spreading and carrying of twenty heaps of dung recorded as a service at Forncett in Norfolk in the thirteenth century. This practice appears to have been commemorated in 1484 when a field is recorded as The Denge, at Great Bardfield in Essex. It was probably an enclosure in which dung was kept.

When not engaged in such unpleasant tasks, or in working fields graphically described (as, for example, Glue Pot – for sticky clay – at Crosby-on-Eden in Cumbria), medieval farmers could apparently look forward to finds of treasure. A field called Goldhorde is recorded in 1251 at Wytham, Berks, and several others are known. Silver in field names however often refers to a fresh water source.

The names of villagers often have an evocative ring – Ralph Jolibody, John Merriman, Gilbert Uncouth, Roger Mouse, John Stoutlook, Agnes Redhead, Evote Wheelspinner, Margaret Merry and Maud Malkynsmaydin are good examples.

Personal names and surnames with Norman French origins can be found from this period on, and there are several English-sounding names which derive from the French. Examples are Grenfell and Greenfield, which have been changed from Grenville.

A large number of personal names derive from the Bretons who arrived immediately after the conquest – Hugh and Alan for example, with their many variants, can be found as both surname and first name.

Although there was a wide variety of personal names in the Middle Ages, it is notable that by the fourteenth century, the names Henry, John, Richard, Robert and William made up 64 per cent of recorded men's names. Other names did not catch on – Alfonsus, Lanfrancs and Conrad for example.

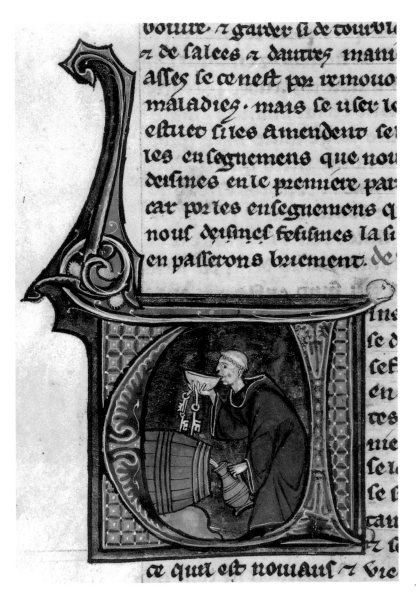

Drunken cellarer, Sloane MS 2435,
f. 44r (British Library)

Occupations connected with the countryside are similarly commemorated through surnames. Thus Warrender or occasionally Warnier refers to an officer employed to watch over a game park. Forester or Forster is self-explanatory, being found as early as 1356. From the lowly cottars are derived the family names of Coterell, Cotter and Cotman.

Other occupations such as Culpepper (connected with spices), Drawater or Knatchbull (literally to fell an ox) refer similarly to jobs, as can Plummer (from a dealer in Plumes or feathers). Brewer, Brewster, Maltmen and Malthus are equally clear of derivation. Walker however, refers to the tradition in weaving of walking (originally trampling cloth in water).

Punishments are commemorated in such names as Brent, Brind and Brennan, referring to a brand or a burning of the hand.

Deserted Medieval Villages

Amajor feature of medieval villages was, paradoxically, the fact that many were deserted at an early date, leaving little but crop marks or enigmatic bumps under fields. Since most successful villages are now still flourishing and the medieval structures have long since been submerged under brick and tarmac, it is the failed examples which are most readily available for study.

From the late 1940s historians and archaeologists have collaborated in studying the remains of such deserted medieval villages (DMVs). There are over 3000 in England alone, with comparable examples in Scotland and Wales (though many of the considerable number in the Scottish Highlands belong to the nineteenth-century Clearances).

When the first studies were made, it was assumed that English villages were deserted as a result of the Black Death in the fourteenth century. It is now known however that this was but one of many contributory factors.

In the Norman period for example, castle building may have led to the depopulation of some villages. The establishment of royal hunting forests certainly called for tracts of land which came under royal forest law, leading to a corresponding drift out of villages in the area.

Documentary sources suggest that much of the peasant population of northern England was wiped out by William I's 'Harrying of the North' in 1069–71 and that numbers were not re-established fully until the end of the Middle Ages.

Many of the 'new villages' founded during the earlier thirteenth century were on marginal land, and while this may have been able to support the inhabitants in times of prosperity, in times of shortage such land proved too unproductive. In 1341 the *Nonarum Inquisitiones* records that taxes were not being paid on account of poor soil and bad weather.

A further phase of depopulation happened in the late Middle Ages, probably as result of the enclosure movement and the gradual switch from arable to sheep farming. The late medieval demand for wool meant good profits whereas arable farming was labour intensive, and due to the diminished population, labour was scarce and wages high. The idea that grasping landowners simply evicted peasants from their villages is however an over-simplification, since by this time there were a growing number of freeholding peasants. Many chose to move out of the villages of their own accord to start sheep farming in the adjacent countryside.

The process of village desertion did not stop at the end of the fifteenth century. Intensive enclosure in Elizabethan England led to the abandonment of some settlements, and emparking – the creation of large estates for noble families – led to further desertions in the seventeenth and (more particularly) eighteenth centuries. A deserted village, for example, lies under the parkland at Attingham Hall in Shropshire.

OPPOSITE ABOVE: *The deserted medieval village of Walworth, Co. Durham, from the air (Cambridge University Committee for Aerial Photography)*

OPPOSITE BELOW: *The deserted medieval village of Ludborough, Lincs, from the air (Cambridge University Committee for Aerial Photography)*

4 · The Church

OPPOSITE: *Canterbury Cathedral, the nave, begun 1379 (Edwin Smith)*

THE CHURCH was of paramount importance in the Middle Ages, and there is consequently a large amount of surviving material that relates to ecclesiastical matters. Religion influenced everything that people did to the point where the secular was continually mixed with the religious – hence the fact that it was not thought sacrilegious to hold markets in cathedrals, to meet there to have chats with friends, or to adorn sacred buildings with grotesque and sometimes obscene carvings. The medieval world was small, and beyond its limits lay a boundless, remote and dangerous expanse. Just as people did not doubt that such a terrestrial world existed, they had no doubts about the hereafter.

Heaven and Hell were as real as the place in which they lived, and faith was not required since it would have implied the possibility of doubt. Life was short and usually not very pleasant, but at the end came everlasting life, and Christ would save all who repented of their sins, however often they sinned, and however late they repented.

The fear of eternal damnation and the hope of eternal bliss were the driving forces that motivated all, lord and peasant alike.

The Church was one of the richest and most powerful landowners in the country. The clergy were organized, like the rest of society, in a rigid hierarchy, and influenced politics and government. Following the Norman conquest, bishoprics and abbeys became feudal baronies and most bishops and abbots were tenants-in-chief, establishing sub-tenants on their lands.

Until the fourteenth century clerics who sat on the great council were representatives first and foremost of the papacy, which had an authority superior to kings and whose influence and wealth spread across Europe. They defended the liberty of the Church while still being tenants of the King, and were able to exercise a curb on royal despotism. Kings ignored the counsel of the archbishops of Canterbury and York at their peril. The collaboration between William the Conqueror and his Archbishop of Canterbury Lanfranc strengthened his hand, just as the opposition of Archbishop Anselm to William II weakened the latter's.

Perhaps the most famous battle between Church and Crown was personified in Thomas Becket, Archbishop of Canterbury, and Henry II. After four of Henry's knights murdered Becket in his cathedral, he was canonized, and almost at once became a cult figure. Henry did penance in Canterbury, allowing monks to scourge him, and promised to go on a crusade. The Crusades indeed were, at least ostensibly, driven by Christian motives.

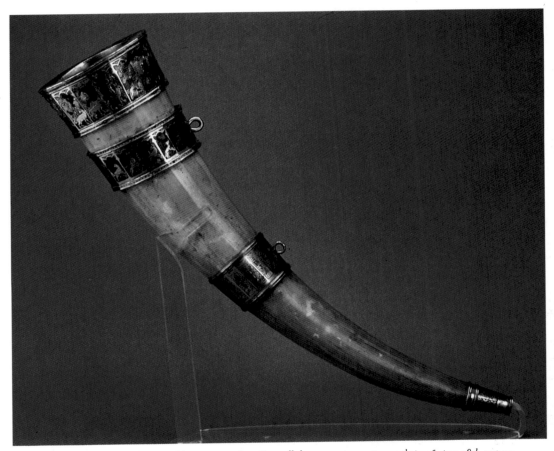

Savernake horn. 12C elephant horn, used by forest wardens. Enamelled mounts 1325–50, mouthpiece fittings 18th century
(British Museum)

OPPOSITE: *Farmer chasing a fox with stolen goose. Early 13C carving on a capital in Wells Cathedral*
(The Dean and Chapter of Wells)

Clerics were a driving force behind major political movements. For instance, Stephen Langton was the intellect behind Magna Carta, and Archbishop John Stratford led the opposition to Edward III. It was not fortuitous that the first liberty defended by Magna Carta was that of the Church. On a more humble level the peasants paid their dues and confessed their sins to the parish priest. In the relatively secular and multi-cultural society of modern Britain it can be difficult to comprehend the strength and uniformity of attitudes and beliefs of the entire medieval population.

From the middle of the fourteenth century the power of the Church started to wane and it was less respected by society. One factor behind this may have been the schisms that divided the papacy, another was the fact that senior clerics had become royal 'yes men', being seen as powerful landowners and grasping tax gatherers.

Patronage

The building of churches and monasteries would not have been possible without patronage. Kings, nobles and merchants vied with one another in enriching churches, for here lay one route to salvation. Westminster Abbey allegedly took a tenth of Edward the Confessor's revenues, and Henry III spent the equivalent of the State's income for two years on it between 1245 and 1272.

In some cases, work ceased when a patron died. This happened when Edward I expired during the construction of Vale Royal Abbey in Cheshire. Major abbeys depended on substantial endowments but were also financed by diverting the revenues of parish churches. In 1363 the revenues of the parish of St Thomas were destined to make repairs to Salisbury cathedral.

The secular clergy were far removed from the world of cathedrals, bishops and monasteries. The upper echelons of the clerical establishment were, by the fourteenth century, made up of men who had served in high office in the court, who were aristocrats, or who had seen papal service, and who were rewarded with a major see. Men of learning seldom rose far, and diocesan experience seldom led to a bishopric.

The parish clergy were similarly unsuited to their task. Many were totally ignorant, and all were given their livings by their feudal overlords, who saw that they could reward their servants with a benefice which would provide a tidy income from tithes and other emoluments without forcing them to dip into their own pockets.

If one ecclesiastical benefice was insufficient to provide an adequate stipend, a plurality was arranged. Anyone could be made a parish priest provided a patron was prepared to appoint him, and the patrons ranged from the King and lay magnates through abbots and university colleges to minor secular landowners. This system of a lay patron bestowing a living on the incumbent still exists today, albeit nowadays a relative formality.

It was not impossible for one cleric to be Archdeacon of Shetland, Provost of Beverley (in Yorkshire), Rector of Wearmouth (Tyne and Wear), Prebendary of Lincoln Cathedral, Precentor of Lisbon Cathedral, and Prior of the Priory of St Agnes at Ferrara (Italy) – indeed, one was.

On the proceeds of the benefice, the holder could sometimes even afford to pay someone to attend to the cure of souls. The benefice might yield £50 per annum, of which the priest might be paid £5, leaving a useful £45 in hand. By the end of the thirteenth century, manuals were being produced to explain their responsibilities to parish priests, and bishops were sending them on crash courses on pastoral duties.

Church Buildings

There are currently some eighteen thousand churches managed by the Church of England, a very large number of which are at least partly medieval. The fluctuating fortunes of churches show in microcosm the fortunes of the neighbourhood – churches were added to or rebuilt in more splendid form when communities grew richer and larger, or were reduced in size when villages shrank and there were fewer parishioners.

The church at which a bishop officiates is known as a cathedral. Most but not all of these are large and magnificent. Generally speaking they are sited in towns rather than villages.

Church art was often sumptuous and included wall paintings and coloured windows, monuments, brasses, fonts and other fittings. These are discussed in chapter 10.

Since parish churches served several functions, their fittings reflect changing elements in ritual and observance. A feature of Norman churches, often removed at a later stage in their history, was an apsidal or semi-circular end. These churches were frequently built on a cruciform plan, with a tower over the crossing. In the late twelfth and thirteenth centuries the expansion of the population led to the addition of aisles. Early aisles were narrow, later examples wider.

In the thirteenth century too the apse or short chancel was replaced by a larger square-ended extension. These chancels had a priest's door in the south wall, and contained the graves of important personnages, who were now commemorated by elaborate tombs, by tombstones or monumental brasses.

In the thirteenth century, the chancel was often lengthened to provide more space for ceremonial processions and for the choir. This meant the high altar was further away from the congregation and a door was made in the south of the chancel for the officiating priest to enter, and seats (sedilia) were sometimes provided for him and a deacon and sub-deacon in the choir.

THIS PAGE AND
OPPOSITE: *Biblical scenes
and decorative motifs on
13c glass, Ely Cathedral
(Patrick Reyntiens)*

Southwell Minster, Nottinghamshire, started before 1174, in the French Romanesque manner (Jenny Laing)

Southwell Minster, leaf on chapter house capital, c.1330 (Philip Dixon)

In the fourteenth century nave walls were heightened and a clerestory (a row of windows in the upper part of the nave wall) introduced to bring light into the nave. The aisles could be wider, as they now had separate roofs. By the later medieval period the aisled nave of four or five bays became common, with transepts and a chancel arch leading into a three-bayed chancel.

A device found in some churches, for example at Lyddington in Rutland, was the use of accoustic jars — pots that were buried under choir stalls or sometimes in walls to improve the sound.

Church Architecture

Churches vary considerably in size and splendour, their plans usually reflecting the fortunes of the neighbourhood. Their architecture underwent a number of styles which can be used to provide dates for their erection.

The Romanesque style   This was first seen before the Conquest in such buildings as Edward the Confessor's Westminster Abbey, and became widespread after 1066 until the time of the Angevins, though churches continued to be built in the Anglo-Saxon style.

The ecclesiastical architecture of the Normans is best exemplified by their cathedrals. They were of exceptional length, with the feature, derived from continental Europe, of an elevation with three levels — arcade, gallery and clerestory. Cathedrals had a wall-passage at clerestory level, in which were the windows that brought light into the soaring buildings. The interior was divided up by piers, with attached shafts. Romanesque arches were round, and the columns and masonry solid. Good examples can be seen at Winchester (where the transepts are Norman), Ely, Norwich and Peterborough.

An important step forward was taken at Durham, where the architect pioneered rib vaulting. This was first tried (prior to 1104) in the choir, and later employed in the rest of the cathedral. Oddly, although a few later buildings such as Lincoln also employed rib vaulting, it was an idea that only became fashionable on the Continent, initially in Normandy, and was one of the elements developed in French Gothic architecture.

Another feature of twelfth-century Romanesque architecture in England was the development of new types of ornamental detail, such as chevron, diaper and billet moulding. Some of these details can be seen in Durham, on the columns.

The twelfth century saw the building of a new choir and crypt at Canterbury cathedral, and in south-west England cathedrals such as Tewkesbury and Gloucester displayed a fourth storey in what has been called the Giant Order.

The Early English style   For long the styles of English medieval architecture were simply labelled 'Gothic' which was essentially derogatory, since it took its name from the barbarian Goths who invaded Europe in the fifth century. By the early nineteenth century it was realized that the different medieval styles should be distinguished, and the style that coincided with the reign of Henry II was termed 'Early English' or 'First Pointed'. In the Early English style the windows were tall and narrow, without mullions, with a pointed, as opposed to a rounded, top.

The starting point for the style was the choir of Canterbury cathedral (after 1174), which was designed by a French architect, William of Sens, in the French Gothic style.

In south-west England, the Early English style was first employed at Wells cathedral (commenced in the 1180s), which had a lot of the solidity of the preceding Romanesque. The style went through a 'transitional' stage in some northern English buildings, where elaborate shafts and mouldings were developed.

The vault came into play again in Lincoln Cathedral, begun after 1192. Ribbed vaults, mouldings and multiple shafts were all employed at Lincoln, and the idea was taken up in the choirs of Beverley, Worcester and Ely. By the mid thirteenth century windows were grouped together to allow more light, and facades were starting to employ multiple lancet windows as part of their effect.

Decorated   This name is slightly inapt since the Decorated Style is in fact no more nor less ornate than any other. It is chiefly the windows which prompted the original classification, being varied and rich in comparison to those of the Early English style. It was in vogue especially towards the end of the fourteenth century, during which time a large number of experiments were made with architectural details.

Bar tracery is a feature of Decorated windows, which are divided into several lights by the use of mullions (vertical bars). Other features include sharp, ornamented spires and complex vaulting.

The style was first used in England in Westminster Abbey (after 1245) and the difficulties encountered in combining such details with other decorative features were eventually overcome with the development of the Perpendicular style.

Perpendicular architecture   The mid fourteenth century saw the beginnings of the Perpendicular Style of English Gothic, giving an increasingly light and airy atmosphere to buildings. The characteristic feature of the style was the use of tall piers with vertical subdivisions, cusped arches, and tall windows with vertical tracery and with geometric patterns filling the void at the top.

A particularly satisfactory innovation was Perpendicular vaulting. English architects had long been innovative in their experiments with vaulting, finding fascinating challenges in the arrangement of ribbing. The star vault was developed in the Early English phase, and involved adding short ribs between the long to produce star shapes. It is well exemplified in Lincoln and Exeter Cathedrals, the latter dating from the mid fourteenth century. The net vault had ribs arranged to form triangles and lozenges. Ribs proliferated in the Perpendicular, and were combined with the webbing between into complex patterns. The fan vault evolved sometime after the middle of the fourteenth century.

OVERLEAF LEFT: *Norwich Cathedral, completed 1145, with 15C spire (Philip Dixon)*

OVERLEAF ABOVE RIGHT: *The 12C Cistercian abbey of Fountains, with its later 15C belltower (Stephen Tobin, first published in* The Cistercians, *Herbert Press 1995)*

OVERLEAF BELOW RIGHT: *Wells Cathedral, west front, c.1230–55 (Patrick Taylor)*

The effect of the most elaborate fan vaulting was of pendant cones of masonry. This can be seen in a late form in Henry VII's chapel at Westminster Abbey, which takes the fan vault into the sixteenth century.

The Perpendicular style is displayed in a diversity of buildings from cathedrals to parish churches. Major buildings in the style include the nave of Canterbury cathedral and King's College, Cambridge, the latter founded by Henry VI. The Oxford Divinity School (incorporated now in the Bodleian Library) and Magdalen College quadrangle are in the same style. Among many parish churches can be singled out three in Suffolk, at Lavenham, Long Melford and Southwold.

OPPOSITE: *Fan vaulting in the cloisters of Gloucester Cathedral (Edwin Smith)*

Archaeology of Parish Churches

The documentary sources for church building are very sparse prior to 1250, and comparatively meagre until about 1560.

The Ancient Monuments Act of 1913 specifically excluded churches, and little attention was paid to their archaeology for the first half of this century. In the past two decades however attention has been focused on the excavation of parish churches, which has led to a much greater understanding of their development.

Church excavation poses problems of its own, due to extensive disturbance by burials and the limited areas available for investigation except in abandoned churches. Finds are few, and due to the re-use of building materials dating can be difficult, although mortars and timber can sometimes be dated firmly. Excavation also reveals only ground plans. Diagonal tooling on masonry points to a post-Conquest date.

A surprising amount is still unknown about medieval churches, but archaeology can shed light on the use of timber building for example. Only one totally medieval timber church survives, in Cheshire. Archaeology can help to answer questions such as whether there is continuity of use from the Roman period, or whether pagan sites were taken over for Christian usage.

The excavation of cemeteries and graveyards is informative about the population of medieval Britain and its illnesses and mortality rate.

Archaeology can also shed light on the changing architecture of a church and the fortunes of its parish. This is well exemplified by the church at the deserted medieval village of Wharram Percy, Yorks (see p. oo). Excavation inside the church showed that an eighth century timber church was replaced probably late in the same century by a stone church, to which a chancel was added. A late Saxo-Norman tower was then added on at a later date. All this mirrors population growth. After the Norman Conquest the Percy family became the local lords, and a major building programme was instituted in the twelfth century. In the thirteenth, the expansion of the population led to the addition of an aisle on the north side and a chapel.

The village then began to decline, so the church was reduced in size by removal of the side aisles. In the seventeenth century the chancel was shortened and it became derelict by the mid twentieth century.

A similar story is unfolded through studying the results of the excavation of St Mary's in Tanner St, Winchester, the history of which

Lavenham, Suffolk, 15c church porch (Jenny Laing)

closely reflected the fortunes of the adjacent streets. St Mary's church began in the tenth century and incorporated a secular edifice, perhaps belonging to a thegn who founded it. It seems to have remained a private church, evidenced by the single doorway opening onto a private plot. Excavation also revealed the position of a rood screen and the altar, as well as a probable font base.

Pilgrimage

Pilgrimages were an important route to salvation, and also a pretext for travel. Their objects were the major European shrines. To see a fragment of the True Cross or some threads from Christ's robe was to come into immediate contact with the fountain of faith. Only slightly less awe-inspiring were the corporeal and incorporeal relics of a saint.

Pilgrims travelled recognized routes, stopping off at established sanctuaries where lesser relics might be viewed. In hierarchical terms Jerusalem came top of the list, followed by Rome. Then came Santiago de Compostela, the Shrine of St James in Spain. England too had its share of pilgrim destinations: outstandingly popular was the Canterbury shrine of St Thomas Becket who had been murdered in the cathedral due to an unfortunate remark by Henry II (see p. 81). Pilgrims there are documented from as far afield as Aberdeen and northern France. Walsingham, in Norfolk, had a famous statue of the Virgin and a replica of the house where Christ was supposed to have lived as a child.

These holy places hosted pilgrims from the international circuit; others, such as the shrine of St Alban or the Shrine of St Edward the Confessor in Westminster, were of more local appeal.

To prove they had visited a shrine pilgrims bought lead or pewter badges. Cast in moulds from which several could be made at a time, these insignia are ubiquitous medieval finds. Two-handled lead pilgrim flasks for holy water or oil could be sewn onto hats or clothes, worn round the neck, and also opened and sprinkled on fields. The badges were sold at booths outside the shrines and show a great diversity of designs. Tokens were also produced for travellers. Again of lead, they include the Boy Bishop tokens. Lead pennies and groats were issued and presumably could be spent in local markets.

An important function of relics concerned their uses for curing physical ills. Shrines kept records of 'miraculous' cures that had been effected, and offerings were given to them by those who felt they had benefited. These included miniature votive models of afflicted parts of the anatomy. At Exeter wax moulded models of limbs were suspended over the tomb of Bishop Edmund Lacy (d.1455), while apertures were left in the shrines for the afflicted to put the arm or leg through to touch the tomb. Ambulatories were constructed round shrines, to facilitate the flow of pilgrim traffic.

Pieces were frequently broken off shrines, and water used for washing saintly corpses was prized. It is reported that St Hugh of Lincoln tried to steal part of the arm of Mary Magdalene by biting a piece off

Pilgrim flask, Southampton (Southampton Museum)

it at the monastery of Fécamp in France. In France too the relics of St Foy were stolen and taken to Conques, where they were incorporated into a magnificent anthropomorphic (i.e. in human form) shrine.

Monasteries

One of the major developments of the Middle Ages was the rapid spread and growth of monasteries, of which there were over a thousand in England. They flourished in England and Wales until the Dissolution by Henry VIII (between 1536 and 1540), when they were demolished in a major campaign of vandalism not since paralleled.

In Scotland monastic destruction followed the late sixteenth century Scottish Reformation.

Monasticism originated in the later Roman Empire, and was introduced to Britain by St Augustine at the end of the sixth century AD. Such early Anglo-Saxon and Celtic monasteries were different from the claustral types that spread with the Normans and their successors.

Monasteries were a retreat for those who wished to withdraw from secular life and devote themselves to God. It was not an easy life:

When you wish to sleep, they wake you, when you wish to eat, they make you fast. The night is passed praying in the church, the day in working, and there is no repose but in the refectory; and what is found there? Rotten eggs, beans with their pods on, and liquor fit for oxen.

Many were located in rural situations, sometimes on marginal land, to isolate the monks from the rest of society; others lay outside towns. As well as being extensive land holders, they furthered education and administration.

A religious house occupied by monks was a monastery; by nuns a nunnery. The community was a convent, a term applied equally to both. They could be either abbeys or priories depending on whether they were presided over by abbots, abbesses, priors or prioresses. Priories were of lesser status than abbeys, and were usually offshoots from them. Houses of friars and houses of Carthusian monks, although also sometimes called priories, are termed friaries and charterhouses. Some abbeys and priories were occupied by canons living under a monastic rule – regular canons. Cathedrals were frequently served by secular canons.

Monasteries vary considerably in details but share basic architectural frameworks in which a routine of worship and work was carried out. Their layout varied according to the order, the particular observances and the site, but generally speaking they were built on level ground and comprised a church, a burial ground, a cloister which was an open square bordered by a covered walk (alley), and various ranges of buildings, which included domestic accommodation. Additionally, there were agricultural estates to provide their food.

A day in the life of a medieval monk   The general pattern of monastic life is seen by considering Archbishop Lanfranc's timetable

*Melrose Abbey, Roxburghshire,
founded 1136 (Jenny Laing)*

(horarium) for the eleventh century Benedictine cathedral monastery at Canterbury. Lanfranc was an Italian and one of the great Norman administrators, having himself been a Benedictine monk.

The day began about 2.30am when the monks assembled for psalms and prayers and then the first service, Nocturns. The next service was Matins, after which the monks waited till dawn and Prime, read in the cloister until 8am when they returned to the dorter (dormitory) to wash and change their shoes before the next two services, Terce and Morrow Mass. Following Mass, a chapter from the order's Rule was read (in the chapter house), before the monks dispersed to read or work until noon. The next two hours were taken up with the services of Sext, High Mass and None.

At 2pm they went to the frater (dining room) for the main meal of the day, before spending the afternoon in work or study. At 5pm it was Vespers, after which they donned their night shoes for a return to the frater for a drink before a short reading in church and the last service, Compline.

Bed-time was at about 6.30 or 7pm. Lanfranc wisely advised that the reredorter (lavatories) should be checked at the end of the day, lest a monk had fallen asleep in there.

Monastic Orders and their Spread

From the first monasteries (founded by St Benedict at sixth century Monte Casino near Naples) a proliferation of others developed. Many had offshoots for females (see below).

The Benedictines The Benedictine Rule dictated every detail of monastic life. The first of over a thousand post-Conquest Benedictine houses built in England before AD 1200 was at Battle Abbey, Sussex, with monks from France. Others include Tewkesbury, Evesham and Malmesbury, all richly endowed by Norman lords. Some, such as Chester or Gloucester, became cathedrals. In Scotland, Dunfermline abbey was founded around 1074, and a Benedictine house was established on the site of the Celtic monastery at Iona in 1203.

The Cluniacs   The Burgundian abbey of Cluny developed its own regime in the late tenth century. The resulting Cluniac Order encouraged art, architecture and learning, and the priories are often of exceptional beauty.

Paisley Abbey in Renfrewshire and Crossraguel Abbey in Ayrshire, Bermondsey Abbey in Surrey and Pontefract Abbey, Yorkshire, are all Cluniac.

Cistericians   The Cistercians were the most important of the 'reformed' Benedictine orders, founded at Cîteaux in 1098 and expanded rapidly in the twelfth century, encouraged by St Bernard. The Cistercians stressed the importance of poverty, sustained by faith and love. They emphasized the balance between physical labour, meditation, and church service. Their churches were austere, decorated only with white plaster, and they wore white habits, in contrast to the black of the Benedictines.

St Bernard did not approve of art: 'Sacred images,' he said, 'form the pavement that we walk on: here one spits on the face of an angel, there the features of a saint are effaced by the feet of the passers-by … to what purpose are these ridiculous monsters, this deformed beauty and beautiful deformity?'

The Cistercians banned warm hoods, bedspreads and combs, all signs of weakness by this time permitted by the Benedictines. No villeins were to work on their lands.

The first Cistercian house in England was founded at Waverley, Surrey, in 1128–9, but the Harrying of the North had created a desirable desolation, so the North became popular for new sites. The monastery at Rievaulx, Yorkshire, was founded in 1131, and from here a daughter-house was established in Scotland in 1136 at Melrose, Roxburghshire. In some cases the Cistercians achieved solitude forceably – at Valle Crucis near Llangollen in Wales, for example, they evicted the villagers from Llangwestl.

Cistercian lands (granges) were tended by lay-brothers, not tenant farmers as in the case of the Benedictine Order. These lay-brothers were generally illiterate, worked in silence except where work made it essential to speak, prayed together at the start and end of the day, attended Mass thirty or forty times a year and on Sundays, and received Communion only seven times a year. Despite the physical hardship, the life of a lay-brother seemed an attractive career to men of humble origin.

By the end of the twelfth century the Cistercians were seen as grasping property developers farming sheep and exporting the wool to Flanders. By the time of Richard I, the Cistercians offered to contribute the revenue from a year's wool production towards his ransom from captivity in Austria. Richard tried to cream off the same amount again, and John was not idle in trying to soak them. They financed their business by borrowing — for example from the famous Jewish moneylender, Aaron of Lincoln.

Augustinians and Premonstratensians   The Augustinian Order was developed specifically to provide extra-claustral work. Basing their Rule on that of St Augustine of Hippo (d. around 430), they renounced personal possessions and preached in the outside world. So too did the Premonstratensians, named after their first house at Prémontré. This drew heavily on the Cistercian Order in framing its regulations. They were known as 'white canons' after their habits, while the Augustinians were 'black canons'. Both were 'canons regular' because they followed a rule (*regula*).

Most premonstratensian houses were founded in the later twelfth century.

Carthusians   Named after La Grande Chartreuse in France, the Carthusians were very strict. Their monks lived in individual cells, and obeyed a vow of silence, meeting only for services and meals. There were Carthusian houses at Witham, Somerset, and Mount Grace, Yorkshire.

Franciscans   In the thirteenth century there were many popular religious movements in Europe and the cult of relics and a belief in miracles became rife. It was into this world that St Francis of Assisi came, a rich Italian who sold all he possessed for a life of poverty and simplicity. In 1209 he founded a new order, the Franciscans. The followers (known as friars), individually renounced worldly possessions, but the order was permitted the accumulation of property.

Friars were essentially missionaries who lived in friaries, often on the edge of towns. They were highly educated and influential preachers. A group of Franciscans concentrated in Oxford, making its university a leading centre for learning in Europe. By the early fourteenth century there were fifty-three Franciscan priories in Britain, including three houses for women — the 'Poor Clares'.

Dominicans   A second order of friars was named after St Dominic. The Dominicans or Order of Preachers were associated with the Inquisition, a Continental movement founded to discover and suppress heresy, but never introduced to England. By the end of the thirteenth century they had forty-eight houses in England.

Minor Orders   The priory of the Austin canons at Walsingham was a major centre of pilgrimage and the Gilbertines were an order of extremely pious nuns.

Ecclesiastical Knights

The Templars (the Poor Knights of Christ and the Temple of Solomon) were a religious military order established at the time of the Crusades (pp. 14–15) in order to protect Christian pilgrims from the Muslims. They eventually became so powerful through the secrecy of their affairs and their accumulation of lands, that their grand master was burned at the stake in 1314 by order of the Pope.

The Knights Hospitaller (Sovereign and Military Order of the Knights Hospitaller of St John of Jerusalem) originated in a hospital for sick pilgrims in Jerusalem. They gained much wealth, operating from Cyprus after the fall of Acre in 1291, and continue their work today.

Nunneries

Nuns were recruited from rich families – women from humble backgrounds had to work, and their kin could not afford the dowries necessary to secure a career as a bride of Christ. Although there were some rich and substantial nunneries in the south (it was said that if the abbot of Glastonbury could marry the abbess of Shaftesbury, their heir would have more land than the King of England), most were small priories, concentrated in the Midlands and North.

Nunneries provided a variety of functions in medieval society. For one thing, they offered a career for women who otherwise would have done little with their lives, and a career which, in medieval terms, represented the highest ideal to which a person could aspire. They also provided accommodation for boarders – widows, or the wives and daughters of men who were away from home, who their menfolk felt would be safer in a nunnery than in their own house. Nunneries frequently needed the boarding fees, but as the boarders often came with maids, pet dogs and sumptuous wardrobes, and chatted to the nuns about worldly matters, they were a source of concern to bishops who tried, without success, to discourage the practice.

Nunneries also occasionally provided schooling, and distributed alms. As major landowners, they provided work for considerable numbers of lay people of both sexes. By the thirteenth century the ideal of St Benedict that the nuns should do much of the manual work themselves had gone by the board, and some of the larger establishments employed a male cook as well as a brewer, baker, dairywoman and laundress. Some nuns even employed personal servants. Such wealth was however exceptional, and nunneries tended to be extremely poor.

As the Middle Ages wore on, educational standards declined. By the fourteenth century Latin was tending not to be understood, and by the fifteenth even French was no longer understood and some abbesses could not read their own foundation charters. Similarly, the observance of the services became lax – nuns came late and slipped out before the end, or gabbled the services quickly in order to get through them faster.

To fill the time thus saved there were the three Ds – dancing, dresses and dogs. The latter were not the only pets kept – monkeys, squirrels, rabbits and birds were also popular, and on occasion taken into church. As for fashion:

Occasionally a wretched bishop flounders unhandily in masculine bewilderment through something like a complete catalogue of contemporary fashions in order to specify what nuns were not to wear. Synods sat, archbishops and bishops shook their heads over golden hairpins and silver belts, jewelled rings, laced shoes, slashed tunics, low-necked dresses, long trains, gay colours, costly materials and furs. (Power, E. *Medieval Women*, 1964, 98)

Nuns also liked to get out and about – one is recorded,

who on Monday did pass night with Austin friars at N'hampton and did dance and play lute with them in same place till midnight and on night following passed night with Friars Preachers at N'hampton, luting and dancing in like manner.

Part of the problem lay in the fact that many nuns found themselves cloistered without having any real vocation. Bishop Alnwick of Lincoln in the fifteenth century had to deal with the problem of the cellaress of Gracedieu, Margaret Bellers, who

... goes out to work in autumn alone with Sir Henry [the chaplain], he reaping the harvest and she binding the sheaves, and at evening she comes riding behind on the same horse.

Another nun, Agnes Perry, from St Agnes, Stamford, ran off with a wandering harp player, while at Cannington in Somerset a visitation found in the fourteenth century that one Joan Trimelet was pregnant – 'but not indeed by the Holy Ghost'. Maud Pelham and Alice Northlode had been holding assignations with two chaplains in the nave of the convent church. The prioress had been above such carnal acitivities, being preoccupied with simony (the buying and selling of ecclesiastical preferments).

Rievaulx Abbey, North Yorkshire, founded 1132 (Annabel Taylor)

Monastic Buildings

The overall layout of the medieval monastic complex basically involved a series of courts, incorporating the cloister and its ranges (which could be said to be the innermost), with the inner court with its granaries, guest accommodation, bakehouse, brewhouse and gate.

Beyond lay an outer court (which contained the farm buildings, and which was reasonably accessible to outsiders), and further out still were the estates, notably the granges which were run as farms. There has been very little archaeological work on the inner and outer courts, and relatively few granges have been investigated.

Rievaulx Abbey Documents drawn up at the time of the Dissolution shed light on the layout of this abbey at that time, and describe a total of twenty-seven buildings in the inner and outer courts, water meadows and pastures. They mention three mills (one a smithy with hammers powered by water and one a fulling mill), a tannery, bakehouse and kiln-house, and offices belonging to the plumber, tanner and smith, a brewhouse.

In the Outer Court there was a well-house, two gatehouses, a guest house and the houses of tenants, who included corrodiars. The latter were pensioners who had made endowments to the monastery. Good examples of corrodiars' houses can be seen at Crossraguel Abbey, Ayrshire. Some monastic precincts survive defined by earthworks, such as at Thornton Abbey, where the precinct extends to 29 hectares (about 72 acres).

Monastic churches   The most important and largest building of any monastery was the church, and the Normans introduced a new liturgy that was reflected in architecture. Over the centuries most churches have been modified or added to.

Most Norman churches were cruciform, with a choir beneath the crossing or the east end of the nave, with the main altar to the east in the presbytery. The transepts evolved out of the side chapels found in Anglo-Saxon churches. At the west end of the choir was a (pulpitum) screen with two altars, forming a space known as the retrochoir. To its west was a second (rood) screen which partitioned off the monastic part of the church, with a nave altar against it. Other altars were located in the transepts or at the east end behind the high altar.

Corrodiars houses, Crossraguel Abbey, Ayrshire (Lloyd Laing)

The Cistercians simplified this plan, building large aisled naves to accommodate the lay brothers, with a short east end, while the canons preferred unaisled naves and long presbyteries. The Knights Templar built circular churches, modelled on that of the Holy Sepulchre in Jerusalem. One such was excavated at Temple Bruer in Lincolnshire.

The liturgies observed were often complex: in Lincoln cathedral an inscription set into a slab of Purbeck marble in the floor directs, *Cantate Hic* (intone here), and was one of twelve processional stopping places, chosen for its accoustics.

Cloisters   The cloister was first used in England in Dunstan's monastic reforms of the mid tenth century. The Late Saxon *Regularis Concordia* called for a refectory, dormitory, cloister, chapter house, warming house, kitchen, bakehouse and guest house. The first cloister we can identify is at the Saxon monastery at Glastonbury, separated from the church by a cemetery. The cloister attached to the south side of the nave of the church first appeared in Edward the Confessor's abbey at Westminster, but became the norm thereafter.

The cloister alley was used for study, and was frequently equipped with carrels or desks, but the open arcades were cold and draughty in winter, and from the fourteenth century were sometimes fitted with glass windows. The cloister alley could also contain a library, and in the west alley of an Augustinian house there was a laver, furnished with water and drains, where laundry might also be done in wooden tubs. The laver was often quite grand, on account of the spiritual symbolism of washing. At the east end of the north cloister was a processional door into the south wall of the church.

Norton Priory, Cheshire   Few complexes of claustral buildings have been investigated in the recent past, but at Norton Priory, Cheshire,

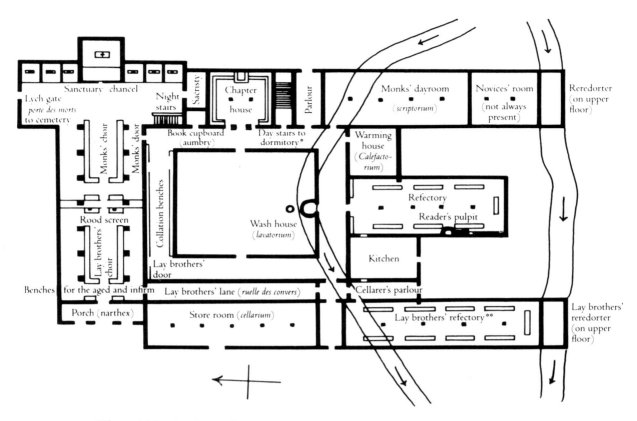

Labels on plan (reading order):

Lych gate *porte des morts* to cemetery

Sanctuary chancel

Night stairs

Sacristy

Chapter house

Parlour

Monks' dayroom (*scriptorium*)

Novices' room (not always present)

Reredorter (on upper floor)

Monks' choir

Monks' door

Book cupboard (aumbry)

Day stairs to dormitory*

Warming house (*Calefactorium*)

Rood screen

Collation benches

Refectory

Reader's pulpit

Lay brothers' choir

Wash house (*lavatorium*)

Lay brothers' door

Kitchen

Benches for the aged and infirm

Lay brothers' lane (*ruelle des convers*)

Cellarer's parlour

Porch (narthex)

Store room (*cellarium*)

Lay brothers' refectory**

Lay brothers' reredorter (on upper floor)

*The monks' dormitory lay over the entire east range   **The lay-brothers' dormitory lay over the entire west range

Plan of a typical Cistercian abbey

excavation showed that the first buildings were of timber, and lay outside the area where the permanent stone buildings were put up. At first the stone buildings were modest – an east range with a monks' dormitory over a sacristy-cum-library, a chapter house, and an undercroft (the day room). The south range contained the frater or refectory. The west range had the outer parlour and cellars on the ground floor and the accommodation for the prior and the guests on the first floor.

Everyday facilities   The east range of a typical monastery extended from the transept, and contained the dorter or dormitory, which had on its first floor a door which gave access to the transept by way of the night stairs. In the later Middle Ages wooden partitions created privacy in separate cubicles.

In Stamford, the reredorter (lavatory) drain contained the remains of a laboratory – fragmentary glass distillation equipment, crucibles and beads of mercury, sulphur and copper, which may have been for alchemy or medicine (see pp. 159–160). On the ground floor of the range a door gave access to the sacristy (entered from the transept) and the library, entered from the cloister alley. Next to it lay the parlour, where conversation was permitted, and then the chapter house. The day-stair gave day-time access to the dorter.

A dormitory undercroft at Rievaulx was excavated in the 1920s, where the contents of the room had been preserved by a roof fall. It seems to have been lit by hanging lights in each bay, and on the floor were found rosary beads, buttons, pens and styli for writing on wax tablets, pewter plates and coins. It was probably originally used as a warming room, later a day-room for working and writing.

The south range contained the refectory, which had a dias at the end furthest from the door, for the senior members of the community, and raised platforms along the side walls for benches and tables. At Fountains Abbey the bases of stone table legs still survive. A pulpit was provided for readings throughout the meals. In early Cistercian houses the frater was parallel to the cloister walk, but by the end of the twelfth century was located at right angles to it.

Food was originally vegetarian, but from the fourteenth century onwards meat was introduced into the diet, and a second meat kitchen was often built, usually attached to the infirmary. Dovecotes for providing a source of meat are known at a number of monasteries; that at Thornholme Priory has been excavated.

The west range of the cloisters was the 'secular' part of the monastery, in front of which lay the great or inner court and gatehouse. The gatehouses were often quite splendid, to impress the outside world. Examples survive at St Andrews and Arbroath in Scotland; in the latter case the vaulted gatehouse is equipped to take a portcullis and heavy doors, and there are vaulted buildings attached.

Precinct walls sometimes survive, for example at Sweetheart, Dumfriesshire. In the west range the cellarer maintained contact with the outside world, buying and selling, which being time-consuming allowed him some exemptions from services. Here too the almoner distributed to the poor the left-over food collected in a basket at the end of a meal. When a monk died, a cross was laid on the table where he had sat, and the food served as usual, but was then collected at the end of the meal and given to the almoner to distribute to the poor, with the request that they prayed for the soul of the dead monk. This was maintained for thirty days.

The range also included the outer parlour, where lay visitors were received, and the guest accommodation.

Infirmaries are to be found at a number of sites – Rievaulx or Easby in Yorkshire, for example, or Waverley.

Carthusian monastery plans were different in that the monks lived apart. At Mount Grace Priory the monastic cells were in fact two-storey houses, each set inside a garden 15.3m (50 ft) square. On the ground floor four rooms were divided by wooden partitions, the living room furnished with a fireplace. The upper floor was given over to study and contemplation, and was glazed. The cell was furnished with piped water, and a latrine.

Gardens The gardens excavated at Mount Grace had individual layouts. Cell 8, for example, had rectangular beds divided by paths made with roof slates, the plants bedded in pits or trenches dug into the clay and filled with heavily manured soil. Cell 9 however was laid out more like a knot garden, with square flower beds edged with stones.

In other orders communal gardens were equally important. Denny Abbey had a cistern for watering the plants, and at Hull where again the subsoil was heavy clay, trenches had been dug in a formal design and filled with compost.

Water supply   The water supply was an important element in monastic design, and the pipe work was often sophisticated, with cisterns and both lead and pottery pipes – a series of jointed pipes was found at Glenluce Abbey, Wigtowns. Wooden pipes have sometimes been found, for example at Beaulieu Abbey. Taps are not infrequent finds, sometimes with a spout in the form of an animal head, or, in the case of Lewes Priory, a human one. Complex piped water supplies first appeared in the middle of the twelfth century. Water was filtered, sometimes through a tank with a pierced grille. At Westminster Abbey a lead cistern was set in a cupboard and used a settling tank, with three pipes through the base; one a feed source, one a service pipe to a tap fed from the cistern, and the third an overflow pipe.

Latrines   Latrines were flushed with through water. At Rievaulx the latrine block was three storeys high, with an upper floor latrine with probable partitoning. At Christchurch, Canterbury, there was seating for 55 monks at a time, at Lewes, 30. Urine was too valuable to pour down a drain, and pots (termed jordans) were made with a handle and round hole to collect it in, as it was used in tanning and in the production of vellum. A jordan could also be carried under the habit for relief during a long service.

Apart from communal latrines, there were individual ones in different parts of the monastery. Monastic drains were often substantial, and have given rise to stories of secret passages from monasteries. The conduit of St Andrews cathedral priory is about half a mile long, and has been traced under houses, gardens and roads in the modern town.

Guest houses   Some guest houses have been excavated, for example at Kirkstall Abbey, Yorks, where there was a group of buildings associated with a large thirteenth-century hall, originally timber-framed but rebuilt in stone in the latter part of the century. Extensive repairs and alterations were made throughout its life.

Granges   The outlying granges sometimes represented monasteries in miniature, with a chapel and domestic ranges round a cloister, and with agricultural buildings in a separate enclosure. This was the case with some Cistercian granges, such as that excavated at Gorefields, but for the most part granges looked little different from secular manors.

Some granges were specialist – Fountains and Rievaulx had stud farms, and Fountains also had a grange at Bradley concerned with pottery production. At Levisham in Yorkshire there was a sheep ranch which belonged to Old Malton.

OPPOSITE ABOVE: *Romsey Abbey, Hants, silver gilt incense boat, c.1350 (Victoria & Albert Museum)*

OPPOSITE BELOW: *Dolgellau, Gwynedd, silver gilt chalice & paten, c.1230–50, probably made for Cymer Abbey (Royal Collections, photo National Museum of Wales)*

The Jew's House, Lincoln,
typical of 12C burgess housing
(Lloyd Laing)

5 · Towns

IN THE RIGID SOCIAL SYSTEM of the Middle Ages, towns acted as a dynamic catalyst for many developments. They also provided employment, markets and a degree of social mobility. It is notable that as the Middle Ages progressed urban populations slowly grew at the expense of the rural.

Towns offered a wide variety of trades and occupations, leisure pursuits and amenities. The bishops, the king and the nobility dominated Norman towns, but rich merchants became increasingly important – by the thirteenth century the burgesses had become key figures.

Towns enjoyed special rights and privileges extended through charters from the king, and through the cathedrals and churches they played an important role in the relationship between Church and State.

Many modern towns retain their medieval layout, and several (of which the old Roman towns of Chester and York are outstanding) retain medieval buildings – a testimony to the prosperity of their citizens who were able to build to last. Town walls were built for both defence and status, enclosing a variety of public and private buildings originally built in wood, but increasingly using brick and stone.

The Development of Medieval Towns

Medieval towns were small by modern standards. Very few towns in Europe housed more than 10,000 inhabitants and most had populations of less than 5,000. London had 40,000–50,000 inhabitants, and the really 'vast' European cities such as Florence, Brussels or Ghent numbered between 50,000 and 100,000 dwellers.

The word 'town' itself comes from the Old English (Saxon) 'tun', which denoted the enclosure round a house and yard, or encircling an estate, but came to be applied to any group of people and buildings within an established boundary. It is preserved in a large number of placenames (Barton-on-Humber, Cassington, Charlton, Oxton etc). The word 'borough' (also found in many present day placenames: Middlesborough, Farnborough and so on), comes from the Old English 'burh', meaning a defended settlement, and was the name given to the towns of later Anglo-Saxon England. Towns were virtually non-existent in Scotland or Wales before the time of the Anglo-Norman advance, and Scottish towns in particular grew rapidly in the later eleventh and twelfth centuries.

The Normans were not on the whole great town developers: their habit of laying waste areas of existing Saxon towns to build castles was however tacit acknowledgement of the importance of the sites themselves. Their developments were mostly confined to practising some borough colonization to establish communities of traders within towns.

The Normans introduced French as the language of commerce, and a major factor of town growth after the Conquest may have been the revival of the trade in luxury items such as fine cloth and wine. As the eleventh and twelfth centuries progressed, some new towns were founded, and some 'old' towns started to expand. In Devon, Domesday Book records only four towns with a fifth showing signs of emerging, but by 1238 there were eighteen boroughs sending representatives to meet the king's justices.

The twelfth and thirteenth centuries were the key period of urban development in Europe as a whole, when the whole system of international trade burgeoned, as well as a network of more local commerce.

Administration

Towns came under the general jurisdiction of a reeve, usually termed a port reeve, whose job was to collect revenue such as tolls and taxes from the town. His rural counterpart was the shire reeve, hence the word sheriff.

The port reeve also headed the town judiciary, and acted as an intermediary between the citizens and the king, should it be necessary. The port reeve was an official established in Anglo-Saxon times, and generally the Normans saw no reason to change town administration.

From the beginning of the thirteenth century onwards the town was normally controlled by a *communa* – a body of elected officers, a mayor and aldermen. The town council evolved from this somewhat later. Towns were designated cities if they possessed a cathedral, though this definition has become somewhat elastic in later times.

The active members of a town were the burgesses, who normally had a house within it (a burgage plot) and probably strips in fields outside, as well as rights to use the town common pasture. They paid rents for their plots and customs to the crown, but they also raised the levies on those entering the walls to trade. They formed the port moot, which met several times a year to discuss matters of common concern to those living in the town. As well as this core there were of course other inhabitants, without the same rights and dues.

Urban amenities   Generally, towns were arranged so that certain zones were given over to particular activities and, in the later Middle Ages, antisocial crafts and activities such as butchery, fishmongery and tanning were banished to the peripheries. Smiths and potters were also marginalized, on account of the fire risk. Sometimes there was specialization in streets. Thus an Italian visitor to the Strand in London remarked that in a single street there were fifty-two goldsmiths' shops,

so rich and full of silver vessels, great and small, that in all the shops in Milan, Rome, Venice and Florence put together I do not think there would be found so many of the magnificence that are to be seen in London.

13c iron barrel padlock key, Billingsgate, London (Lloyd Laing)

Friaries and hospitals were important elements in town planning, with hospitals (lazar houses) being located well outside town confines. The lazar house in Cambridge was in a far corner of the borough, and that at Exeter was located half a mile outside the city gates.

Suburbs were mainly occupied by the poor, though sometimes with a few rich houses. Nearly a third of the population of medieval Winchester lived in the suburbs.

Guilds

Guilds could be formed for a variety of different reasons and were essentially groups of people co-operating for particular objectives. Two main groups of guilds can be distinguished; those that were socio-religious, and those concerned with trade.

Guilds were organized societies which made rules for their members and regulated their conduct. They had officers, and kept strict accounts. The guild members paid agreed fees, undertook to worship at a designated church, chose an alderman to lead them and stewards or wardens to administer their accounts. They met yearly and spent money on candles for the church, funerals for their members, ale for their yearly festival and charity for the poor and needy.

Guilds also financed building programmes – for example forty guilds allied at Bodmin to rebuild the church between 1469 and 1472. In Coventry and York guilds provided hostels for poor pilgrims. A guild in Worcester repaired the walls and bridge of the city, and guilds in Worcester, Ludlow and Bristol provided free schooling.

Socio-religious guilds did not make much impact on society before the thirteenth century, and were to come into prominence in the fourteenth to sixteenth centuries. They became rich in some cases, and were believed to be financing dubious heretical causes, so they were suppressed by Acts of Henry VIII and Edward VI, which sequestered all their funds.

Craft guilds controlled the work of their members, regulated the quality, pegged prices and controlled the employment of apprentices and the hours to be worked. They also intervened in disputes, and defended the interests of their craft against rivals. There were many craft guilds in each town. In the fifteenth century there were around sixty in York, and Bristol (which was smaller) had twenty-six. Some guilds pressed for wage increases for their employers, and organized strikes, though such associations were frequently banned by town authorities.

Related to the guilds were associations of merchants who traded in the same commodities, such as the Mercers in London. Some, such as the Merchant Staplers (who were concerned with the export of wool) and the Merchant Venturers, who dealt in cloth, were involved in international trade.

Merchants

There are numerous accounts in medieval literature of the careers of individual merchants. Although few merchants were people of learning, medieval traders were often people of great piety who endowed churches and monasteries and who also ploughed back some of the profits for the good of the community at large. Much of the major medieval church-building programme was financed by merchants, as is attested by the fine 'wool' churches of the Cotswolds, East Anglia and south-west England. In some churches can be seen the badge of the merchant, or, for example at Tiverton, Devon, carvings of his ships. They also lavished money on church fittings, and funded public buildings and monuments, such as the market crosses of Chichester and Salisbury, on schools, on hospitals and on almshouses for the poor. Collectively, merchants financed splendid guild halls.

Many merchants' lives are 'rags to riches' yarns. Godric of Finchale came of humble farming origins in Norfolk, but broke away to become a pedlar, first in his own district, then further afield. He joined forces with some others, and then started trading with Scotland, Flanders and Denmark. With some of his partners, he bought a half-share in a ship, and then a quarter share in another. He bought cheap and sold dear, and after sixteen years in trade went on a pilgrimage to Compostela in Spain, returning to become a hermit at Finchale. When he died in 1170 he was proclaimed a saint.

Another successful businessman was Sir William de la Pole, son of a Hull merchant who made a vast fortune from the wool trade, and in the 1330s became rich enough to lend Edward III money. In 1340 he was arrested and jailed for mismanaging the royal finances, but the Parliament of 1344 withdrew the charges. He founded a hospital outside Hull, and married his daughters into noble families. His son became the first Earl of Suffolk.

Weights, measures and accounting   Weights and measures had to be strictly controlled for the efficient conduct of trade. Life was complicated for merchants because there was no standardization of measurements in Europe, or indeed, in Britain. Some units, such as a 'baker's dozen' or a 'long hundred', could have differing values. To make matters worse, units of measurement were changed from time to time in particular places. Some overall control however was exercized. All cloth for example that came from a specific centre had to have the same number of threads and the same measurements. Towns had sets of measures, and also balances for checking weights, which were subject to periodic checks for accuracy.

Merchants developed methods of calculating their often complex accounts. To this end the Arabic system of numbers was introduced, and the counting board, on which counters known as jettons were

moved around, came into operation as a primitive form of computer. Sets of jettons were manufactured – gold for the rich, silver for the less rich, copper or bronze for most purposes. Tournai was one of the centres which manufactured them. Medieval jettons often looked like coins, which led of course to some being passed off as the real thing.

The Middle Ages saw the origins of some of the most important elements in modern finance, for example, credit transfer. Debts were recorded on tallies – wooden sticks with notches representing the amount owed. These were then sealed by both creditor and debtor and split, each party taking half. When the debt was discharged, the debtor destroyed the tally. Such tallies could also be used as cheques. If a merchant had provided the Exchequer with a bill he was issued with a half tally which he took to the collector of revenue who had to pay the sum indicated when the tally was handed over. Letters of credit were also used by people of known financial integrity to guarantee expenses. Bills of exchange were developed both for international trade and as a kind of traveller's cheque.

Money lending   Money lending was a facet of medieval commercial life, although the Church disapproved of all money that was not acquired through work. Capital investment was acceptable since there was an equal chance of loss, but straightforward money lending was inadmissible. This moral standpoint was not shared by Jews, who thus became the money lenders of medieval Europe. As time wore on, so much money was involved in mercantile transactions that merchants, particularly the Lombards, took on money lending themselves. Eventually even the Franciscan Order of monks found a 'nice little earner', lending money at 10 per cent. Such transactions were however carefully obscured under other names. For coins see chapter 7.

Insurance   Medieval merchants developed this concept, which came into fashion in the fourteenth century, and was mostly restricted to overseas shipping. Premiums were calculated on the basis of the risks, but 18 per cent of the worth of the cargo was not unknown.

Markets and Fairs

Markets were integral to town development, and the granting of market rights was frequently the first stage in the transition of a settlement into borough status. The creation or recognition of markets by the King was particularly a feature of the time of Henry III and Edward I, when town growth was at its greatest. Markets were generally licensed, and the revenue of tolls charged at the town gates and from merchants plying their trade in the town often enriched royal or noble coffers. The term for trading or bargaining was 'cheaping' – hence Edward the Elder granted Taunton the tolls of the 'town's cheaping'. The word has passed down in the form of place names, such as Cheapside in London (where bargaining was done in the street), or Chipping Norton. It also gave rise to the word for a pedlar – a chapman – used down to the nineteenth century (hence chap books, which were books of fairy tales or nursery rhymes sold by pedlars). Most markets were weekly occurrences, but in addition there were annual or biennial fairs, which were also licensed and which raised revenue both from tolls and from the rentals for booths.

The market place was the focus of many towns. Alnwick in Northumberland, for example, has a radial plan centering on the market place and church. In many towns business came to be concentrated on a main street terminating in a market square and a church or market hall.

At the time of Domesday book there were some fifty recognized markets, though the actual number was probably greater. Control was exercised in granting permits for them, for if they were too close geographically they might interfere with each other's trade. In the thirteenth century it was argued that markets should be six miles apart, which gave time for traders to walk there, transact their business, and get home before dark.

In the thirteenth century there were four main fairs in England; at Winchester, Northampton, St Ives and Boston.

Some fairs grew up in connection with the veneration of a particular saint. Some even originated in the cause of charity. Stourbridge fair, Cambridgeshire, was granted by King John in order to raise revenue for a leper hospital, while one at Burley in Rutland was held to raise money to rebuild the town.

Some fairs became well known because they were markets for particular commodities. Hence Goose Fair in Nottingham (which is still a major event each autumn), or Barnet's horse fair, which attracted bloodstock from as far afield as Wales and Yorkshire. In London St Bartholomew's and Greenwich fair were particularly known not for their merchandise but for the quality of the entertainments – plays and side shows.

Sunday trading   Sunday was convenient for markets, but trading was banned from 906. Nonetheless, churchyards were seen as good places to hold markets, and Sundays ideal for holding them, so the law was constantly infringed. In 1285 a statute forbade the holding of fairs in churchyards, and in 1448 Henry VI banned all Sunday trading, 'necessary victual only except'.

Disputes of course were liable to break out, and had to be resolved on the spot. To this end there was assembled a merchants' court known as the court of Pie-Powder (from French *pieds poudrés*, 'dusty feet'), so called because traders came straight from the market place. It was held in a building sometimes called the tolbooth, which was originally a booth where tolls were paid and where weights were tested; later the tolbooth was used as a town hall or a prison (for example in Edinburgh).

Urban Leisure and Pleasure

Although many present day inns appear to be half-timbered 'olde worlde' medieval, very often they are former burgess houses or of a much later date. Some however still survive from the Middle Ages,

Thame hoard, 15c reliquary ring and coins (Ashmolean Museum, Oxford)

The chapel in Vicar's Close, Wells (Patrick Taylor)

perhaps the earliest being the Trip to Jerusalem in Nottingham from which pilgrims are traditionally said to have set off, as they did from the Tabard in London in Chaucer's *Canterbury Tales*. The Trip to Jerusalem appears to have been designed as an inn from the outset, and parts reputedly date back to 1189.

The majority of the surviving medieval inns belong to the fifteenth century, a few more to the fourteenth. The most common conform to the courtyard plan, where the main inn buildings do not face on to the street but are grouped round a courtyard behind it. Accommodation is provided at first-floor level, the ground floor being used as stables. A good example of this type is the George Hotel, Dorchester-on-Thames, Oxfordshire, built to accommodate visitors to the shrine of St Birinus.

The second type is the 'gatehouse' inn, which has a block facing the street with a passageway through it to the courtyard, round which were situated the stables and offices. A classic example is the George Inn at Glastonbury, Somerset, built by Abbot Selwood (1457–93). It was essentially a pilgrims' inn for visitors to the abbey. It has an ornate stone façade, and stands three storeys high, still retaining its original panelling.

Because many of the records of the Middle Ages were produced by the Church there is a tendency to see the period as highly moral. Despite the emphasis on leading an exemplary life however there was a seamier side to towns. Although no brothels survive from the Middle Ages, their existence is recorded in street names such as Love Street in Chester. A lady of the night however is depicted on a medieval pot from near Mincing Lane, London. She is shown being accosted by a client, and the genitals of both figures are clearly indicated. The woman is encircled by a red ring. The couple are shown next to a dog and a man holding a pole above his head and a serpent is also depicted on the pot. The red circle round the woman presumably represents a bath-tub and the figure with the pole may be an acrobat. The animals may be part of side shows.

Brothels were usually located in particular quarters of towns, adjacent to bath houses. From the twelfth century on, these were communal establishments for both sexes, where food and drink could be consumed. The baths were large wooden tubs accommodating several people at a time. If it was preferred, however, a popular option was to hire a tub for two. These bathing establishments were known as stews, and they flourished until banned in the sixteenth century. In London they were on the south bank of the river at Southwark, and the whole region was the entertainment area of the medieval city, known as Bankside. For those of less carnal taste, there were theatres, acrobatic shows, performing animals and bear baiting.

A jug, probably made in Nottingham but exported to Bruges (where it was found) has, on the spout, a more carefully modelled woman wearing a huge brooch and a beard. Her hands are on her thighs, and her divided skirt falls away to reveal her legs. She too is probably a harlot – on the side of the jug knights on horseback are queuing up.

More reputable entertainments sometimes figure in medieval art.

Late 13C pewter tavern token depicting bird, London (Lloyd Laing)

Two drawings by Matthew Paris, now in Corpus Christi Library, Cambridge, show a reception given for Richard, Earl of Cornwall, by the emperor of Sicily. Two female jugglers are shown, both Saracens, balancing on balls of metal and wearing see-through dresses of pale green. One girl has a clapper.

Henry I had a menagerie at Woodstock, Oxford, in which animals including lions, leopards, camels and a porcupine were displayed. The elephant was a particular crowd-puller, as was one given to Henry III by Louis IX of France, which was kept at the Tower of London for four years and was drawn by several artists, including Matthew Paris.

Hygiene

Hygiene was a serious problem in medieval towns. Water was piped or brought by conduit into London, Exeter, Southampton and Bristol by the fourteenth century, and to other towns in the fifteenth.

Garderobes (sewage chutes) were sometimes located over a street. Sewage was piped into a cesspit (or even into a basement cellar) and taken away at night in pipes (barrels) to be dumped in watercourses or on the land. Sewage pits were also dug and when full were covered over with clay. These increasingly fell out of use from the fourteenth century. It was widely believed that disease was spread by odours, so keeping them at bay was deemed important.

A sixteenth century Dutch physician noted of his English hosts that

the neate cleanliness, the exquisite finenesse, the pleasaunte and delightfull furniture in every poynt ... wonderfully rejoysed mee; their chambers and parlours strawed over with sweete herbes refreshed mee; their nosegays finely entermingled wyth sundry sortes of fragraunte floures in their bedchambres and privy roomes, with comfortable smell cheered mee up and entirelye delyghted all my sences.

Winchester, Hants, city gate (Philip Dixon)

Late medieval houses in Cambridge (Philip Dixon)

RIGHT: *Late medieval houses in Tewkesbury, Glos (Philip Dixon)*

Sausage making in a butcher's shop, early 14th century, from MS Douce 5, f. 7 (Bodleian Library)

Large numbers of sewage pits have been investigated in Chester, Plymouth, Winchester, Southampton, Taunton, Winchester, Worcester and York, and botanical and zoological studies have shed light on urban life. Herbs and spices were common – poppy, mustard, mallow, linseed, coriander, caraway, dill and fennel are all represented. Savory and parsley were probably dried.

Studies of the sewage show that grapes, raspberries, blackberries, strawberries, pears, apples, figs, mulberries, bilberries and gooseberries were eaten in appreciable quantities. Urban diet contrasted markedly to that of the country people. In Taunton there were three figs per pound weight in the sewage, suggesting that these fruits were comparatively cheap. In the late Middle Ages they cost 1½ pence per pound – in 1300 a penny was the daily wage for a labourer. It was possible that they were used as laxatives.

Eggs of parasitic worms show that roundworm and whipworm were endemic.

Kitchen waste is frequently found mixed with sewage. Barnard Castle produced 23 kinds of fish and 3 molluscs, 14 species of bird and 14 of edible mammals. Bran and porage residues are common, but there is little evidence for peas or broad beans. Hay and straw was dumped, after use on floors, probably to dull the smell. Moss was used as toilet paper (the first example of the latter in Britain was marketed by the British Perforated Paper Company in 1880).

The most informative sewage pit in medieval England is probably that known as Pit 14 at Cuckoo Lane, Southampton. Good documentation proves it to be the pit of a prominent merchant, Richard of Southwick. It contained remains of grapes, figs, raspberries, strawberries, sloes, cherries, plums, walnuts and hazelnuts. Other items included pottery from France, lustreware from Spain, a Near Eastern jar, a bucket bowl from eastern Europe, Venetian glass, Iranian silk, rope and string of palm fibres. It also included the remains of a Barbary ape. We know from the documents that the household consumed various meats, used pewter at table, and liked music.

Public latrines were constructed at London, Leicester, Hull, Southampton and Exeter. Such conveniences could also be private assets. In Brook Street, Winchester, an apparently public-spirited citizen provided a series of public latrines, the ulterior motive behind which was the collection of urine for the fulling (cloth bleaching) industry which he operated on his premises.

Rubbish pits also contribute to understanding life in medieval towns. At Southampton the bones from twelfth-century pits indicate that butchery and possibly also stock keeping occurred within the town – the remains sometimes include whole carcasses. By the thirteenth century the size of joints was reduced but the range of cuts became more varied, pointing to specialist butchers. Similarly, twelfth century pits do not produce the range of botanical remains of later periods.

Medieval Pottery

In Medieval Britain wood and leather were used for many more purposes than they are today, including for the manufacture of platters and bowls, the latter being turned on the lathe. Many examples of wooden vessels have turned up in excavation, for example at Threave Castle, Kirkcudbright, at York and at Southampton.

Pottery was most often used for the production of jugs and cooking pots, though a wide variety of other vessels can be encountered, such as fish dishes, bung-hole cisterns, lamps, jordans (urinals) and watering pots. Ceramic was also used for roof-furniture, not only for glazed roofing tiles and ridge tiles but for ornamental finials and chimney pots, and additionally for curfews, which look like giant casserole lids and were used for putting out fires.

The traditions of later Anglo-Saxon pottery continued into the Norman period – from glazed Anglo-Saxon Stamford ware evolved beautifully-glazed lustrous dark green jugs, for example. The heyday of medieval potting was the later thirteenth to early fourteenth century, when jugs were decorated with different kinds of applied and coloured ornament. Some jugs were like later Toby jugs, decorated with amusing human faces, and others, such as the Moot Hall jug from Nottingham, has relief modelling of knights on a hunt. Puzzle jugs, of which the most famous comes from Exeter, were designed with openwork and spouts like straws, only one of which enabled the drinker to consume the contents – unknowing victims found the liquid pouring out of the holes on to them.

Pottery kilns have been excavated in many parts of Britain, and in many cases, such as the kilns at Laverstock, Wilts or Ham Green, Bristol, the products are sufficiently distinctive for them to be recognized in excavations far from their place of origin. Pots from Scarborough, Yorks, for example, were traded up into Scotland and across the North Sea.

Urban Problems

Market colonization tended to be a problem in some towns, where stalls and even shops were erected in the middle of the main thoroughfare. Thus in Stratford-upon-Avon the main street, 90 ft wide, had a row of shops built down the middle.

OVERLEAF: *Medieval bridge, Rushen, Isle of Man (Lloyd Laing)*

Late 13c polychrome Saintonge jug, Kidwelly, Monmouth (National Museum of Wales)

The surfaces of streets were an on-going concern. In Winchester flints were spread over chalk, but here the street rapidly became rutted and choked with rubbish, which instead of being cleaned was topped with a new surface. Eventually, 5 ft of street surfaces (eight in number) built up at Gar Street near the castle.

Citizens were frequently called upon to pay for the paving of streets, to maintain the flow of trade. Andreas Franciscus at the end of the Middle Ages commented about London that,

All the streets are so badly paved that they get wet at the slightest quantity of water, and this happens very frequently owing to the large numbers of cattle carrying water, as well as on account of the rain, of which there is a great deal in this island. Then a vast amount of evil-smelling mud is formed, which does not disappear quickly but lasts a long time, in fact nearly the whole year round.

A number of problems and contingencies led to the building of stone town walls, particularly in the thirteenth century. They were not always defensive, but since they were costly to erect, possession of a wall implied prosperity. During the Middle Ages about 108 towns in England acquired their own fortifications. Coventry's scheme took 200 years to complete, and many remained unfinished. In 1321 Hull began a programme of town defence building to enhance its status. Taxes — murage levies — were raised to pay for the wall building.

In some cases, such as Chester, Lincoln and London, existing Roman town or fort walls were incorporated into the scheme. Where there were existing Anglo-Saxon earth-and-timber defences, thirteenth-century walls often took in new areas.

Between the wall and the main built-up area of the town a road ran round the perimeter of the defences, to allow soldiers and supplies to be brought up to it rapidly in an emergency — a pattern already observable in late Saxon Winchester. The road still survives in a number of towns, for example at Cuckoo Lane, Southampton. Dead-end streets which backed on to the town walls were generally where cheap properties could be found.

The development of the walls to some extent reflects trends in castle building: towers were built at intervals along the circuits to give flanking cover, initially semi-circular, then later D-shaped. By the fifteenth century square towers were being favoured, probably to carry artillery. This also led to the appearance of gunloops in walls, the earliest example of which, datable to *c*.1360, are in Southampton. The walls were furnished with wall-walks, and with crenellations. Where not dictated by other factors, town walls tended to enclose rectilinear or circular areas.

In some cases the town walls were planned along with the castle as a single design. This is apparent at Conway and Caernarvon in Gwynedd, where the walls join the Edwardian castles, and where the towers served to cut off sections of wall should they be captured. The concentric plan developed in castle architecture at this time was imitated in Oxford, where there are two concentric town walls.

Southampton, town wall (Philip Dixon)

York's defensive scheme is one of the best preserved and most impressive in Europe where the walls are somewhat unusually set on top of an earthen bank (the Anglo-Scandinavian rampart that crowned the earlier Roman defences). The gates (which in York are called Bars) predate the building of the wall and had portcullises and barbicans. The portcullis at Monks Bar survives, complete with its windlass.

Town gates, like those in castles, were a focus of attention. At first they were simple retangular towers with a central passageway between guard chambers. At a later stage semi-circular towers were added on to the front, and by about 1350 it was normal to build a gate with two drum towers: one on either side of the entrance passage way. In some towns the chamber above the entrance was put to civic use, as a guildhall or the exchequer.

Late medieval gates were substantial square towers designed for prestige, richly decorated with coats of arms and statuary. They were not always joined by walls.

Town Houses

Most surviving medieval town houses were the substantially built homes of rich merchants and belong largely to the latter part of the period.

Early dwellings were timber-framed with wattle walls, though by the twelfth century some stone building was being employed by the rich, for example at Moyse's Hall in Bury St Edmunds and King John's Palace buildings on Porters Lane and Blue Anchor Lane, Southampton. Some, notably the Jew's House in Lincoln and the Music House in Norwich, are testimony to the importance of Jews in medieval urban economics.

Some houses were very large – the Norman residence on Cuckoo Lane had a street frontage of 17.37m (18½ yds), and ran back 32.3m (34 yds). 'King John's Palace' in Southampton extended to two floors on a quayside, with the ground floor given over to storage and sales. As in Romano-British towns the fronts of buildings in prominent high street positions were usually devoted to shops.

Medieval architects and builders favoured variations on two basic town-house plans, both dictated by strictures of space and the urban priorities other than domestic.

The most common, in order to present a small frontage on to the street, was the right-angle type, which had a gable (called narrow plan) or at most a short wing (broad plan) facing the street. In essence such a plan involved arranging the offices and rooms one behind the other. A good example is Beam Hall, Oxford.

The second plan, employed where space was at less of a premium, had ranges of rooms placed parallel to one another, with a line of shops in the front and a parallel line of domestic accommodation behind, sometimes separated by a courtyard.

In a medieval house the main element was the hall, which was divided by the screens passage from the pantry and kitchens, and which often extended to the full height of the building. Domestic chambers (solars) were located above the screens passage, and were sometimes fronted by a gallery (which could be used by minstrels), overlooking the hall.

A complicated plan is well exemplified by the fourteenth-century Tackley's Inn in Oxford, which is a double range house with a frontage of shops over which are a series of solars which may have been rented out with the shops. This front range also has an undercroft. Behind, the hall is parallel to the frontage, and extends to its full height. The hall was entered by a passage through the shops. The variation on this, in which the front range was separated by a courtyard, is exemplified by Balle's Place in Salisbury.

By the eleventh century houses were wooden-framed with clay floors, the structural timbers apparently being slotted into sill beams laid on the ground surface.

As in Southampton, the transition to stone building took place in Lincoln in the late twelfth century, and may have been occasioned partly by more stable conditions in the time of Henry II, partly due to booming prosperity. Timber-framing continued to be used during the Middle Ages since it was flexible, and enabled upper storeys to project over the street (jettying). This was the case in such famous medieval streets as the Shambles in York.

In Southampton it is possible to trace the fortunes of particular areas. At first occupation was concentrated in the area to the north and west of the Bargate. From the twelfth century onwards however the prosperous clustered in the south and central areas of the town, with a French colony in the south-west quarter, where French Street now lies.

The urban poor at home Winchester is unusual in providing, especially through excavation, good evidence relating to the homes of the poorer sectors of the community. Brook Street and Tanner Street was a classic example of a lower-class district, with housing and workshops juxtaposed and with its own local church, St Mary's.

The housing in this area in the thirteenth–fourteenth century comprised single-cell buildings, about 3m (10 ft) square, with traces of internal partitioning to divide them into a living area and a bedchamber.

In York there were rows of workers' houses at Goodramgate and there was a tendency to build houses in the churchyards so that the

OPPOSITE: *Late medieval glazed jug, Caerlaverock, Dumfriesshire (Historic Scotland)*

Long-cross pennies of Henry III (Lloyd Laing)

Groat and half groat of Edward III, London (Lloyd Laing)

rents could be spent on expensive church chantries. The Goodramgate cottages had two storeys, with a shared roof (like modern terraced houses), and were timber-framed and two-roomed. The upper storey was jettied over the street. The tenants were probably journeymen.

Scottish and Welsh Urban Life

Neither Scotland nor Wales were urbanized in the way England had been before the Norman Conquest, and there has been proportionately less archaeological excavation. However, recent excavations in Perth, Aberdeen, St Andrews and elsewhere have begun to build up a picture of Scottish urban life.

Perth was founded by David I (1128–1153) and by the twelfth century was defended, probably by a stone wall and wet ditch. Excavated houses were built of timber, and finds from Kirk Close included a fine wooden lavatory seat positioned above a cess pit of the thirteenth–fourteenth century.

Aberdeen was also founded by David I, and grew prosperous through its extensive overseas trade, particularly with Bruges, to which wool was exported. By the fifteenth century it had a population of over 2,000, which was large by Scottish standards.

Excavations have shown that in the late twelfth to early thirteenth century the land bordering the road from the centre of town was divided into plots for houses. The best preserved remains comprised those of a row of houses parallel to the street, with a suggestion of external staircases to an upper storey. Clear areas in front and behind were later used for building.

Both timber and stone buildings of medieval date were excavated in Aberdeen, reflecting the varying prosperity of the occupants. One stone fifteenth-century town house, known as Provost Skene's house, still survives in the city.

In Wales the Saxons had built a burgh at Rhuddlan, but towns did not start to become established until the period after Edward I. Excavations have been carried out at Caernarfon for example, where the town grew up around the castle.

New Towns

The foundation of 'new towns' in the Middle Ages makes an interesting comparison with the similar phenomenon in the twentieth century. Although perhaps not as many towns were founded on virgin sites as historians have supposed in the past, there is little doubt that some measure of deliberate town planning was employed in additions and improvements made to existing sites. This of course was nothing new, for grid-iron street plans were a feature of Anglo-Saxon burghs.

Prior to 1100 the King was the key figure in new foundations. One in three towns was a royal foundation, and 80 per cent were in the shadow of a fortress. In the time of Henry I, half the new towns were close to castles, but more were baronial settlements. New towns established from the late twelfth century onwards did not enjoy the protection of a castle. Some of them prospered, some withered. Among the latter were Moreton-in-the-Marsh, Glos, and Broadway, Worcs.

OVERLEAF: *Ladies in a carriage, from the Luttrell Psalter, Add. MS 42130, f. 181 (British Library)*

Of the towns begun on green-field sites, perhaps the most famous was New Winchelsea in Sussex, which was laid out with a rectangular grid plan when the old town was threatened with destruction by the sea. The encroachment of the waters on the parish church led Edward I to begin rebuilding on top of cliffs. The streets were named Prima Strata, Secunda Strata, etc. (First Street, Second Street).

Salisbury, in Wiltshire, was built to replace Old Sarum which had been the site of Iron Age and Roman settlements. The Normans built a massive ringwork, inside which was a rectangular keep and a cathedral. The site was not well chosen – the soil was unproductive, the town wells were inadequate, and the soldiery came into conflict with the clerics. In 1223 the whole township was moved to a new site on the Avon, on the orders of Bishop Pore. The town was laid out on a chequer plan, with two churches and a market within the town, and a third church outside it. The cathedral, also founded at this time, remained adjacent but independent, enclosed from the fourteenth century by the close wall. Channels were constructed to carry water down most streets, countering the need for wells. By the fifteenth century it was the third most important provincial town in England, and was a major centre for the wool trade.

Waterfronts

In recent years considerable attention has been focused on medieval waterfronts, which archaeology has shown were frequently very substantial. The waterfront development is particularly clear in London, where between 1000 and 1550 land was reclaimed for the construction of a series of docks. In the Anglo-Saxon period inlets from the Thames provided beaches at which merchandise could be unloaded. While these seem to have been used also by Norman merchants, soon a programme of land reclamation began, which involved erecting timber revetments on the foreshore, then filling up the area behind them with dumps of rubbish capped with stone or gravel. At Trig Lane it was found that this revetting was done at two levels, separated by a horizontal plate, allowing the upper level, which was damaged more readily by the tides, to be repaired without having to disturb the lower, submerged levels. Such a system enabled a greater depth of water for the berthing of larger ships.

Just west of Baynard's Castle excavators found a complete dock of the fourteenth to fifteenth centuries, with oak rubbing posts along the stonework to prevent boats being damaged. An unloading platform was also found, with the site of a mooring post. Present-day Thames Street coincides with the line of the early medieval waterfront, and here ran long narrow plots, often with an alley down one side, with halls furnished with stone vaults and cellars for storing merchandise.

Other good examples of medieval docks have been investigated in Hull, Southampton and King's Lynn.

is in nuos mictu?

t testamentum eius.

nt mandatorum

ad faciendum ea.

Ships entering port, Bodleian MS 264, f. 253v (Bodleian Library)

6 · Trade and Communications

THE GROWTH OF TOWNS was closely connected with trade. Although the known medieval world was small, its economic tentacles spread almost halfway round the globe. Overall patterns of industry governed the axes of medieval trade. Industry was concentrated in areas which were given over to the manufacture of particular categories of commodities, and were correspondingly densely populated. The Low Countries and north-east France were such areas, which widened to include north-west Germany and south-east England. Large numbers of skilled craftsmen came to this part of England in the later medieval period, and were an important human resource. The Hanseatic league (see below) was based on the towns of the Low Countries and northern Germany, and influenced the trade from northern Europe. Bruges was the destination of goods shipped from the East by Italian middlemen. In northern Italy and Tuscany there was another major manufacturing area, ideally situated at the hub of Europe and made accessible by existing Roman roads. It controlled sea-going traffic with the Islamic world, and with the eastern Mediterranean lands of Europe.

To facilitate the two-way flow of trade from the core to the periphery, the Italian merchants set up trading outposts. The Italians were both entrepreneurs and manufacturers, producing woollen and silk goods, glass, pottery and metalwork. As a result northern Italy was prosperous, and had the resources and leisure to develop a cultural life which led in time to the Italian Renaissance. To a lesser extent southern France and eastern Spain was a trading region. There were also small pockets centred on particular towns.

Imports

Outside the 'industrial belt' lay a Europe that was primarily concerned with farming and mining. It bought manufactured goods from the industrial regions, and supplied them with food and raw materials. Beyond, in northern and eastern Europe, were areas which depended on fishing and hunting, and which supplied such commodities as fish, furs and timber. The world of Islam provided luxuries, many imported from further east, in return for wool and linen, metals, manufactured goods, furs and slaves.

Excavations in Britain have brought to light finds of Chinese Sung celadon porcelain. Silk, another commodity of Chinese origin, has been found for example in Southampton, where fragments include a piece of samnite probably woven in Byzantium, and a tabby weave similar to the material used in a bishop's travelling cloak found in Nubia.

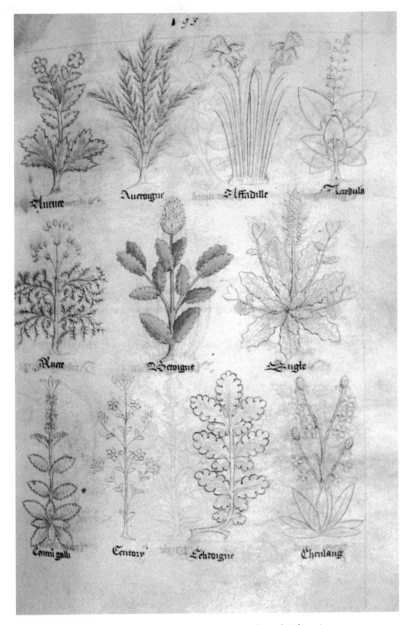

Page from a 15c English herbal, Add. MS 29301, f. 51r (British Library)

OPPOSITE: *Gough's map of England, c.1360, named after an 18c antiquary who first studied it (Bodleian Library)*

The personal seal of Richard of Southwick, 13th century (Southampton Museum)

Spices were deemed essential to enliven medieval cooking, and included ginger, pepper and sugar, which was treated as a spice because of its rarity, and was introduced to Europe by the Arabs. The spice merchants were known as the *grosarii*, hence the modern word 'grocer', named after the *peso grosso*, the heavy beam used by Italian merchants for weighing oriental spices.

Other exotic imports included Islamic glass, such as the famous Luck of Edenhall, and the remains of a barbary ape from Africa, found in the sewage pit of Richard of Southwick in Southampton (see p. 122). From nearer home the complex networks of European trade brought commodities from all over northern, western and eastern Europe – leather from Spain, timber and iron from Russia and the Baltic, wine from France, to name but a few.

Although most food was home produced, fish was imported on occasions, usually from Scandinavia, and wine was brought in by the barrel. Sweet wines came from as far afield as the eastern Mediterranean – Cyprus, Crete, Greece and even Syria. Regardless of where they were produced, they were termed *malvoicie*, 'malmsey', in a butt of which George, Duke of Clarence, was allegedly drowned in the Tower of London in 1478.

Sweet wine was never as popular as dry – figures for Southampton for 1443–4 record that 345 barrels of sweet wine were imported, along with 896 of dry.

The main wine trade was, not surprisingly, with France. The Bordeaux region had been exporting wine to Britain long before 1066, but after the Conquest the trade intensified. French sailors initially brought the wine from Bayonne and by the fourteenth century English sailors also had a hand in the trade. Bayonne vessels are documented in Chester by 1200, and the Welsh ports were also in receipt of Bordeaux wine either directly from France or by way of Bristol. The Irish Sea seems to have been a major axis of trade in French wine. In the thirteenth century pottery from the same area, presumably part of the same cargoes, was being traded from Saintonge and has been found for example at Kidwelly castle in South Wales, in Dublin, Chester, and further north at Glenluce Abbey and Kirkcudbright in south-west Scotland. The finest Saintonge wares were most attractive, with polychrome designs of birds and shields on a white ground, and with elegant profiles with 'parrot beak' spouts. Plain, green-glazed vessels were also traded, along with more decorative jugs from Rouen and elsewhere. In 1372 Froissart documented that some 200 English, Welsh and Scottish ships were loading up at Bordeaux. German wine was not as favoured, but Rhineland products are documented in London from the twelfth century and in Bristol in the fifteenth.

Other luxury products include almonds, dates and figs, oranges, raisins and currants, rice and olive oil, all of which came from the Mediterranean. From Spain came bonnets, girdles and leather gloves (Cordovan leather was particularly prized). Swords, glass and cutlery emanated from the Rhineland and from Italy came armour, gold, silver, jewels, silks and cloth-of-gold fabrics.

On a more mundane level, iron, steel, pitch and hemp came from

Miniature 14c copper alloy barrel padlock, Norfolk (Lloyd Laing)

Scandinavia. English longbows used at Crécy and Agincourt were re-putedly made from wood from the Carpathians, though yew for bows was also imported from Spain. Cotton, used in the manufacture of candle wicks in Candlewick St in London (and elsewhere) came from the Levant. Cloth was imported – cambric from Cambrai, arras from Arras in France, 'fyne cloth of Ipre' from Ypres, and Fustian (which takes its name from the Italian word fustango) from Italy and Flanders. Even vegetable seeds (especially onion) were imported.

Exports

Britain in turn exported foodstuffs to regions with less areas of fertile farmland. Grain was exported to Scandinavia, Gascony and on occasion to Italy. English cheese was much prized abroad, and Scottish salmon competed with Russian caviar in the luxury market of Europe. Cloth was exported from England from the fourteenth century, and English embroideries, already famous in Anglo-Saxon times, were fashionable in Europe. Other exports included lead and tin, coal, daggers, buckles, leatherwork, meat, honey, herring and alabaster carvings from the Midlands, especially Nottingham. Sheep were both imported and exported for breeding.

Coinage

William the Conqueror found a very sophisticated monetary system in place in England – more developed than anywhere else in Europe. He therefore copied the weight and fineness of later Anglo-Saxon pennies, and struck a succession of eight coinages mostly with facing portraits (in contrast to the profiles favoured by Edward the Confessor) and a cross as the main design element on the reverse, along with the name of the moneyer and the mint. Mint names continued to be given on coins throughout the medieval period, though moneyers names were dropped in the time of Edward I. Many of these moneyers had Anglo-Saxon names. William I's last coinage had the letters of the word PAXS (peace) in angles of the cross. Some of these were badly made, but were not as inferior as those of William II and Henry I, who has the distinction of striking the worst coins ever produced in England. As a result they were easy to imitate, and forgery was rife. A charter passed against forgery in 1100 (or 1103) and action taken in 1108 did nothing to stop the rot. In 1124, so the *Anglo-Saxon Chronicle* relates, 'the penny was so bad that the man who had at market a pound could by no means buy therewith twelve pennyworths'. The solution found was to collect all the moneyers together at Winchester and test their products. Those found guilty of malpractice or forgery were castrated and had a hand amputated.

The later issues of Henry I were officially nicked at the edge, to prevent traders cutting them in half to ascertain that they were solid. Normally halfpennies and farthings were produced by cutting pennies in halves and quarters, which is relatively easy to do with sharp scissors, as the coins are very thin. The long-cross pennies of Henry III

Toothache. Early 13c carving on a capital in Wells Cathedral (The Dean and Chapter of Wells)

had a long voided cross which facilitated this cutting, and very large numbers of fractional coins of this issue have been found.

The anarchy of the reign of Stephen led barons such as Eustace Fitzjohn and Robert de Stuteville to issue their own coins. The coins of the former depict an armed knight, the latter the same on horseback. Some of Stephen's coins were defaced on the die — possibly to prevent the dies being used by the enemy, if they fell into their hands. Other coins bear the legend PERERIC, which is meaningless, perhaps with the deliberate intention of producing an anonymous coinage. Around this period coining began in Scotland, with issues of David I and of Henry, earl of Northumberland.

The first coins of Henry II were extremely crude, and weakly struck, and are known as 'Tealby' pennies after a hoard of 5,127 of them found in 1807 at Tealby in Lincolnshire. In 1180 however Henry invited Philip Aimer of Tours to design a new coin. This was the short-cross design, which had a facing bust on the obverse and a short voided cross in a circle on the reverse, with quartrefoils in the angles. These coins may look crude, but in point of fact medieval coins were designed for fast and efficient die production. The bust was not intended as a portrait but a symbol of royalty, and the legend proclaimed that the king was Henricus Rex, regardless of whether it were Henry II, or his successors Richard I, John or Henry III, who all used the same type. The designs were composed by using a minimum number of hubs to build up composite letters, and the whole operation was fast and efficient. Henry III introduced a gold penny tariffed at 20 silver ones. This coin, produced by William, the king's goldsmith, was intended as a rival to the issues of gold florins in Florence in 1252, which rapidly gained currency in Europe. It had a full length enthroned portrait of the king, a fine example of Gothic numismatic art. It was not adopted by later rulers, and the coins are extremely rare. Clipping the coins (trimming the edges for silver which was then collected and melted down) was prevalent, so Henry III introduced a new long-cross coinage with the arms of the cross extended to the edge of the coin — if all four ends of the cross were not visible on a coin, it was illegal. Responsibility for all the coinage was given to the King's brother, the Earl of Cornwall, on a 50 per cent share of the profits divided between him and the King.

The Hanseatic league   Trade in northern Europe had been mostly in the hands of merchants from Scandinavia and the Low Countries, but some cities in north Germany allied to take over some of this business, and became in the thirteenth century the Hanseatic League. From 1207 King John entered into trading agreements with merchants in the Rhineland and the Netherlands, and at this period English pennies became common currency in Utrecht and elsewhere. Henry III entered into negotiations with the Holy Roman Empire, both political and economic, which led to trade treaties including an English declaration of liberties to the merchants of Cologne. English wool was exported to Westphalia where it was made into cloth. Between 1228 and 1240 English pennies, which are common in Westphalian hoards at this period, were widely imitated in Westphalia, the copies being struck by clerics and local counts. In 1240 English merchants, who felt their privileges were being threatened, forced Henry to withdraw his support for the trade, and the flood of English coin abroad and its imitation there stopped until 1250, when there was a fresh wave of imitation. The largest series seems now to have been struck in the Netherlands, notably Brabant, where the copies substituted a garland of roses for the king's crown on the obverse. As a result they were known as 'rosarii', and somewhat surprisingly turn up in large quantities in southern Scotland. They were banned by Edward I in 1299, but were soon replaced by copies which were closer to the originals, and which even included imitations of Scottish coins.

Penny of John, short-cross coinage (Lloyd Laing)

Further currency developments The saga of imitation continued, its fortunes fluctuating with that of the wool trade.

Edward I began by striking short-cross pennies of traditional design, but in 1279 he introduced a new design which was to remain standard for all silver coins to the end of the Middle Ages. On the obverse was a facing, clean-shaven and youthful 'portrait': on the reverse, a long cross with groups of three pellets in the angles. Although the mint name still appeared, the names of the moneyers were removed, as all the coins were the responsibility of one man, the Master of the Mint. The only exceptions to this were a few coins struck by the Abbot of Bury St Edmunds, who had the moneyer's name, Robert de Hadleie, on the reverse. The new coins were struck at a variety of mints, the names of which appeared on the reverses.

In Scotland Alexander III paralleled developments in English design, but abandoned the short-cross reverse of his predecessors William the Lion and Alexander II in favour of a long-cross, first used *c*.1250. With the appearance of Edward I's new long-cross coinage, he introduced a new profile portrait on the obverse and a long cross, similar to Edward's, on the reverse, only with pierced stars (mullets) in the angles, the number of points on the mullets probably being a code for the mints, since the coins did not bear a mint name. This coinage was probably first struck in 1280.

Sterling of William the Lion, sterling of Alexander III, first coinage, Lanark mint, sterling of Alexander III, second coinage (Lloyd Laing)

Edward I also introduced a silver groat (fourpence), which was short lived, and silver round halfpennies and farthings.

The next innovation came with Edward III, who introduced the first regular gold coinage in 1343. Two Florentine goldsmiths, (Kirkyn and Nicholyn were the names given them in England) were made joint Masters of the Mint, and issued a florin (tariffed at six shillings), and its half (called a leopard) and quarter (termed a helm). The designs were superb, the half and quarter taking their names from the main type on each. The Latin text on the florin was one used on amulets, and was seen by the superstitious as a method of preventing clipping. In 1344 the florin was replaced by a noble, valued at 6/8d, with an obverse design of the King in a ship – perhaps an allusion to the English victory at Sluys in 1340. No half or quarter nobles were struck at this time, but were issued later.

In the middle of the fourteenth century the English coinage ran into

Edward II penny

trouble, partly due to the importation of the large numbers of foreign imitations of English pennies, popularly called 'lusshebournes', as many of them came from Luxembourg. The penalty for importing these coins was hanging and quartering.

As a measure to control the coinage the Trial of the Pyx became a regular feature. By this process, examples from every journeyweight of coins were placed in a sealed casket (pyx) at the end of every three months, and sent for checking. A secret mark was employed by the Mint Master, to keep a check on output, and the study of these 'privy marks' as they are termed lies at the basis of the classification and dating of later English medieval coinage. Devices in the design included the use of broken letters, or rings (annulets). Under Edward III the mint was opened at Calais, and this operated intermittently, producing a large coinage under Henry VI.

The other main innovation was the new gold coinage of Edward IV. He introduced a Ryal or Rose Noble, tariffed at ten shillings, but as the old noble was the standard professional fee (like the guinea later on) a new coin tariffed at 6/8d was introduced, called an angel – its half was termed the angelet. The angel had George and the Dragon on the obverse, probably an allusion to the triumph of the House of York over that of Lancaster, and on account of this design was regarded as very lucky. The angel was used by the Tudors and Stuarts in the ceremony of the king's evil – the sovereign touched the coin, which was pierced and given to lucky recipients suffering from 'king's evil' (scurvy) to wear as a prophylactic. Angels continued to be struck specially for the purpose after they had gone out of general use.

In Scotland, Edward III's groats and halfgroats were paralleled by issues of David II, first struck in 1357. These like the pennies had a profile bust. A facing bust not dissimilar to the English appeared on the coins of Robert III. David also copied Edward's system of privy marks. Scottish coins were worth less in England – in 1374 four Scottish pence were worth three English pence. By 1390 the Scottish groat was only worth twopence in England, and later still the ratio became twelve Scottish pence to one English.

The first Scottish gold coin was a 'demy', issued by Robert III around 1393, which imitated the French gold écu of Philip VI of Valois, struck between 1328 and 1350, a forceable reminder of the strong ties between Scotland and France known as the 'Auld Alliance'. One other Scottish coin is worthy of particular attention. This is the groat of James III, with a three-quarter bust, issued about 1485. It was the first true portrait on a Scottish coin, and probably the earliest Renaissance portrait outside Italy.

There was one further period in which foreign coin was pouring into Britain. This was in the late fifteenth century, when Venetians were engaged in active trade. The Venetian galleys brought large numbers of base coins, known in England as galeyhalpens, or Galley halfpennies, which were circulated quite widely due to the shortage of small change. The importation began around 1400, and they were initially used by the Venetians to pay for wool. In 1416 pressure on the Venetian Senate banned galeyhalpens being exported at source, but they still managed to evade the port controls, and turn up in hoards down to the sixteenth century.

Ships and Shipping

Some consideration is given to the evidence for medieval ports and quays in chapter 6. Not surprisingly, finds of boats are rare in archaeology, though ships are not infrequently depicted in art, for example on coins and seals, and are mentioned in the documentary sources. The artists however often took liberties with the depiction of sea-going vessels, and references in texts are often ambiguous. More information survives from the Continent, where more examples of boats have come to light.

Prior to the *Mary Rose*, a Tudor warship belonging to Henry VIII, the only post-Conquest boat known to survive to any extent is the *Grace Dieu*, built for Henry V in 1416–18 and wrecked in the river Hamble. Although not salvaged, it is partially exposed in the spring tides, and has been seen to have been a clinker-built (i.e. with overlapping planks) vessel, with five thicknesses of plank at every overlap.

The *Grace Dieu* was a type of vessel known as a carrack. Different terms are employed in medieval documents to describe types of boat and ship – navis (ship), galia (galley), batella (small boat), carvela (caravel), balingera (barge) scapha (skiff) and spuranciea (spinace) are all terms used.

Ships descended from those of the Vikings continued to navigate northern waters down to the thirteenth century. They are clearly depicted in the Bayeux Tapestry, and in the iron fittings of the twelfth-century door at Stillingfleet, Kent, which retains the dragon head prow associated with Viking vessels. Such ships are known as 'keels' and were long and low, used as warships.

Two types of vessel are better represented than others; the hulk and the cog. The hulk was a deeply curved vessel without a stern post, sometimes held together with ropes. It was known from the ninth century onwards in Europe, and is depicted on the medieval seal of Great Yarmouth, and on the town seal of New Shoreham (originally called Hulkesmouth). An actual example was found at Utrecht, datable to the twelfth century. A hulk is depicted on the gold angel of Henry VII, struck at the end of the fifteenth century.

The cog was a flat-bottomed trading vessel, used in North Sea waters from the end of the Viking age until the beginning of the fifteenth century, but particularly popular in the fourteenth. It had a very steep stem and stern, to facilitate unloading and loading at high tide, and is depicted on seals and coins, for example on a coin struck at Heddeby in Sweden or on the seals of some of the Hanseatic towns of northern Germany. A virtually complete cog of the fourteenth century was found in the river Weser at Bremen, Germany.

In the fifteenth century the single-sailed ship was ousted by one with smaller square sails atop the mainmast and with small sail-bearing masts fore and aft. Instead of being clinker-built the ships were now

Hulk on an 'angel' coin of Henry VII (Lloyd Laing)

147

built with planks laid edge to edge. The new type of ship is depicted on a bench end in King's Lynn, datable to *c.*1420.

Lighthouses

Three medieval lighthouses survive in part: at St Catherines, Chale, on the Isle of Wight, at St Michael's Mount, (Cornwall) and at Ilfracombe, (Devon). Many others are known from documentary sources, and are found from Aberdeen to Dover and Rye on the east coast and St Anne's Head (Pembroke) and Carn Brea (Cornwall) in the West. They often seem to have been put up through the agency of the Church, and were, not surprisingly, sometimes manned by hermits. The Chale lighthouse stands to a height of four floors, square inside and octagonal outside, with a pyramidical roof. It was lit by a cresset (an open bowl-shaped lamp in which a wick was floated), the light from which shone through narrow slits and could hardly have been very effective.

Probably more effective was the lighthouse on top of the church tower at St Michael's Mount, which has a light in a stone cresset and a pentagonal lantern with glass-mullioned windows.

Bridges

Bridges and fords played an important role in the location of towns and in the axes of roads. Medieval bridges have survived in re-markable numbers, to attest the efficiency of their builders – many still carry heavy traffic. Medieval bridges are characterized by their massive piers and their cutwaters, usually pointed, to deflect the force of the current from the piers. Above the piers are refuges for pedestrians, and the bridges usually have several arches. Some are hump-backed, due to pointed arches. Other small hump-backed bridges have no parapets, and were designed for pack-horses whose loads overlapped the narrow bridge. Late medieval bridges tend to have lost their humps. The arches were produced using wooden shuttering, and the earliest are barrel vaulted.

Later medieval bridges used ashlar ribs, infilled with rubble. Some urban bridges had buildings erected on top of them, for example the famous London Bridge, which incorporated an entire street. Chapels are sometimes found at the end of a bridge, so resident hermits could extract the tolls. Other bridges have fortified gateways, for example Monmouth. Good medieval stone bridges can be seen in Dumfries and Chester.

Timber bridges were also built, and pile driving was employed to create foundations, with a heavy block hoisted on a pulley as the driver or ram. Old Rochester Bridge had 10,000 piles of elm, rammed into the river bed, when it was rebuilt in the late fourteenth century. Coffer dams were also used to keep the water back during building – traces of one were excavated at Waltham Abbey, Essex. A medieval wooden bridge survived at Chepstow down to the nineteenth century.

Caerlaverock, remains of timber bridge in wet moat, c.1277 (Historic Scotland)

Roads

Roads were the arteries of medieval trade. The Romans had created a network of metalled roads which carried military and civilian traffic rapidly across the land. The Anglo-Saxons used at least some of the Roman roads, and also employed them in determining parish and other boundaries. The place name 'Street' (from Latin *strata*) was used in Anglo-Saxon times to denote a Roman metalled road. As the road surfaces broke up, travellers started to use the storm-water ditches that flanked them as hollow ways, but the growth of new settlements resulted in the gradual abandonment of the Roman road system during the Middle Ages and its replacement by alternative thoroughfares. Thus, when Northampton was founded in the ninth century, some distance from the Roman Watling Street, that section of the Roman road was not maintained, and a new by-pass through Northampton created. Some of the Roman roads however were put back into commission in later centuries, particularly the eighteenth.

Some medieval road networks have similarly not survived. Some of these were connected with particular industries, with roads built to transport salt from Cheshire, and others to carry fish from the Wash ports to the Midlands.

The medieval maps of Matthew Paris (*c.*1250) and the Gough map (of *c.*1340) help to show the pattern of roads in medieval England, when coupled with documentary sources such as the accounts of royal peregrinations. By the fourteenth century roads were tending to converge on London again, as they had done in the Roman period, with major roads connecting the city to Cornwall via Winchester, Salisbury and Exeter. Another went to Marlborough and Bristol, a third to Gloucester and on to Wales, a fourth roughly along the line of Watling Street to Lichfield and Carlisle, and the fifth (the Great North Road) through Stamford, Newark and Doncaster, then veering west to Carlisle. Many other major towns had several roads converging on them, notably Chester, Leicester, York, Lincoln, Marlborough, Salisbury, Win-

Iron rowel spur, Lochmaben Castle, Dumfriesshire, mid to late 14th century (Lloyd Laing)

chester, Woodstock, Shrewsbury, Lichfield, Gloucester, Oxford and Windsor.

Roads were generally classified with Latin names, the collecting term being *viae* (cartways) of which the *viae regia* (roads of the kingdom) were open to all travellers. The *communis strata* of legal documents belonged to particular towns or even individuals. Packhorse roads were termed *vici*, and footpaths *itineri*.

The route followed by the cortege of Queen Eleanor, wife of Edward I, can be traced from Lincolnshire (where she died) to Westminster. Edward ordered crosses to be erected at the places where the cortege rested and three survive, at Geddington and Hardingstone in Northants and Waltham Cross in Essex.

With the exception of the kings and some merchants, few people needed to travel widely in the Middle Ages. There is however virtually no written evidence of specific merchant routes, nor any recorded complaints that the kings had difficulties travelling around, even though there are no records of road repairs between the fifth century and the medieval period. The fact that so many Roman roads underlie modern ones does however indicate that roads must generally have been kept in good order.

The lack of written discussion about the kings' travels could mean one of several things: the roads were repaired as a matter of course before the intended journey; the roads were in reasonable condition and repair was so routine as to need no comment; or that travellers didn't bother with roads much but simply took their pack animals across country, using the complex system of trackways around the fields.

GK Chesterton's assertion that 'the rolling English drunkard made the rolling English road,' whilst picturesque, is fanciful, for so often it is clear that English lanes simply follow the lines of what are clearly medieval fields in origin. The fields came first; the roads after, rather than vice versa.

Traces of the medieval communications system are visible as crop marks or bumps and hollows in some medieval landscapes. Routes can be discovered too from old estate maps, where they exist.

13c Jetton, latten metal, used with a
counting board (Lloyd Laing)

7 · Science and Technology, Superstition and Medicine

THE MEDIEVAL PERIOD was one of vigorous creativity and invention, concerned with many of the preoccupations of the later twentieth century — the quest for alternative sources of energy, the conservation of the natural resources that were left, the efficient management of manpower and finances, for example. The earlier Middle Ages in particular were a period of dynamism, optimism and vigorous growth. Prior to the Black Death the population expanded rapidly.

The medieval world is usually regarded as an intellectual wilderness, full of superstition and credulity, which hung on to a few remnants of Classical learning and more of Early Christian cant. Yet although there was much in medieval thought that seems bizarre and even risible to modern minds, it was in medieval thinking that the roots of modern science, technology, and medicine were based.

Certainly the earlier part of the period was highly organized and seen to be a reflection of the Divine sense of order. From the mid fourteenth century however progress started to decline. The population dwindled, class differences became more strictly defined, and there was social unrest which often turned into urban violence.

The later Middle Ages saw the growth of superstition (until the fifteenth century witchcraft was of little consequence) when people turned increasingly to fringe cults, particularly mysticism, for spiritual enlightenment. Society became increasingly permissive, and standards of living declined.

In short, the medieval world represented a foretaste of things to come in the modern world, and in recent years historians have increasingly turned to the period for insights into contemporary trends.

Mechanization

The early medieval period saw a rapid development of industry and technology, on a scale not witnessed since the Roman occupation.

After the Norman Conquest, industry burgeoned, one of the main factors in its growth being the development of machinery.

In the Classical world machinery had been used for mechanical toys and amusements such as the lifting and lowering of scenery in the theatre. In the Middle Ages its potential was developed to take the drudgery out of back-breaking repetitive tasks.

Clocks

The medieval engineering developments involved in producing mechanical clocks paved the way for the innovations of the industrial revolution. They were not merely machines for telling the hours, but were astronomical computers.

One of the key pioneers in clock technology was Richard of Wallingford, a fourteenth-century bishop of St Albans. The son of a smith, he was a compulsive inventor, and developed new approaches in trigonometry as well as an astronomical clock and two astronomical instruments. One of these, the Albion, was used for locating the planets, the other, the Rectangulus, was a device with four rulers hinged to one another and mounted on the top of a pillar with a swivel joint. It was used for taking accurate sights.

The astronomical clock was immensely costly, and regarded by many of his brethren as a mad undertaking. Edward III, who saw it, thought the money should have been spent on the upkeep of the church. The Tudor antiquary John Leland admired the clock around 1540, commenting on how it could be used to look at the course of the sun and moon or the fixed stars, or to regard the rise and fall of the tide.

Mills

A post windmill, from the Luttrell Psalter (Jenny Laing)

Of all the machines in use, the mill was the most widespread. It turned wind or water into cost-effective (and environmentally friendly) energy for grinding flour, tanning leather, processing cloth and a variety of other tasks.

Domesday Book shows clearly the economic importance of mills since it documents no fewer than 5,624: more than a third of the manors had at least one mill. The sites of these mills are mostly known, and many of them seem to have survived into the eighteenth and nineteenth centuries. On the river Wylie in Wiltshire, to take one example, there were three mills every mile along a ten-mile stretch of water.

The mills played an important economic role in society. Although the initial investment was high, the returns were comparable, and consortia were formed for joint ownership. Once a person possessed a mill, it was possible to contest the erection of another that might reduce income. Alternatively, compensation could be paid.

The water mill was developed around the end of the second century BC in the Classical world, but not until the development of gears was the undershot or horizontal water mill a viable proposition.

Powering mills by wind has the drawback that the gusts can come from any direction. While fixed mills may have been satisfactory in the East, where winds are less variable, in western Europe the post-mill was developed, a horizontal mill mounted on a vertical axle which could be turned to be at the right angle for the wind. There are none surviving from the Middle Ages, but their existence is known from excavation.

In the fourteenth century the tower mill made its appearance, in which the part containing the machinery was static, and consisted of a tower, on the top of which was a rotating cap in which the sails were located. A stained glass window at Stoke-by-Clare, Suffolk, shows just such a windmill of the fifteenth century.

Astrolabe, 1326, used to determine time from the altitude of the sun or the stars
(British Museum)

Water mills   Medieval water mills were of all the types found in later centuries: horizontal, undershot and overshot. The horizontal mill had a wheel set horizontally under the mill-house, and this type is found in Anglo-Saxon England at Tamworth as early as the eighth century. It is found widespread in early medieval Ireland, and, it has been suggested, was introduced from North Africa.

Horizontal mills occur in the northern Isles of Scotland, and a working example, probably of the eighteenth century, survives at Dounby in Orkney (they are known as 'click mills' because of the sound they make). Here they have been attributed to the Vikings, but it is quite possible they were introduced previously by the Irish. Although flour was the main commodity produced, mills were also used for forging iron. Two mills in Somerset are documented in Domesday Book as paying their dues in iron blooms, which might suggest that they were being used to forge, the mill wheels being presumably attached to cams operating a trip hammer.

Cams were certainly understood in Europe from the tenth century, and water-driven hammers are documented in Germany at the beginning of the eleventh century. The earliest certain evidence for mills used in this way for ironworking comes from the fourteenth century, at Chingley in Kent.

Fulling   A more common use of the cam connected to a water mill was in fulling – the process whereby the cloth produced on the loom was cleaned and thickened by beating. Archaeological evidence for fulling mills is limited, but one is known at Fountains Abbey.

Fulling mills brought about a minor industrial revolution in the thirteenth century. Originally the work was done by treading and stamping on the cloth, but the cam-driven tilt hammer of the mill was an energy-saving alternative. With the expansion of the woollen industry, mills were sometimes converted from grain to fulling. Lords of the manor sometimes demanded that tenants should bring their cloth to the manorial mill for fulling, just as they had previously insisted that the manorial mill ground all the tenants' grain. Needless to say such practices led to strong hostility on the part of the tenants. In 1274 Abbot Roger of St Albans tried to enter tenants' houses to confiscate cloth that had been fulled in the abbey's mill. The tenants rebelled, set up a fighting fund and had their womenfolk appeal to Queen Eleanor when she visited the town, since it was deemed, 'hard to satisfactorily calm the anger of women'. Unfortunately this was to no avail because Eleanor did not understand any English. An attempt to settle the matter in court found in favour of the monastery.

After fulling, the cloth had to be stretched again, which was done on large frames, a process called tentering (hence the expression 'to be kept on tenter hooks'). This took up so much space that areas of towns were set aside for it. The post-holes of the tenter frames have been found in excavation in Bristol and Winchester.

Floating and tidal mills   Not all water mills were securely constructed on river banks. There were floating mills, and from the twelfth century tidal mills (another medieval invention) are attested. One is recorded at this date at Woodbridge, on the river Deben in Suffolk.

Tidal mills became increasingly popular in the thirteenth century and later. They were constructed on low-lying ground where the speed of the fall of the water was insufficient to power an ordinary mill. To power them, dams were built creating ponds, sometimes many acres in extent, and swinging gates were put up to control the flow of water into the ponds. When the tide turned, the pressure of the water outside closed the gates. When the water level had dropped enough below the mill the gates were opened and the dammed water allowed to rush down the mill race to the water wheel.

Looms   The production of cloth was also improved with the arrival of the horizontal loom, developed sometime in the early Middle Ages, and probably introduced to western Europe from the Near East, by way of Italy. The earliest certain evidence for the horizontal loom comes from thirteenth century archaeological deposits in eastern Europe and Russia. Depictions of treadle looms can be found in thirteenth-century manuscripts, but it is likely that it was developed at least as early as the eleventh century.

The importance of the horizontal loom lay in the fact that it facilitated the production of cloth on an industrial scale, because the length was not restricted by the height of the loom.

Non-renewable Sources of Power

Wind and water resources were unlimited, but others were much less readily renewable. The traditional fuel used in medieval industry was charcoal, which was needed for the extensive iron production. Iron working was immensely destructive of timber. To produce 50 kilos (112 lb) of iron, 200 kilos (440 lb) of ore had to be reduced with 25m³ (32½ yds³) of wood. In forty days, one furnace could eat up a section of forest with a 1km (⅝ mile) radius.

Iron was needed in the Middle Ages not only for tools, but for the arms and armour required for the many wars, and even for building. The octagonal chapter house in Westminster Abbey, built between 1245 and 1255, employed an iron structure not unlike an umbrella to reinforce the walls and prevent them falling outwards. The construction involved iron bars attached by hooks to the central stone column which connected with iron ties in the walls. It was not successful, and stone buttresses had to be used instead.

Wood was also used for tanning, rope making, glass making and building, as well as for producing barrels, table utensils, furniture and of course for heating the home.

As the medieval period wore on it became increasingly difficult to find sufficient suitable timber for the large-scale building operations. For the mid-fourteenth century building programme at Windsor Castle an entire wood of 3,004 oaks was required. Ten years later another 820 oaks were felled in Combe Park and 120 in Pamber Forest for the same enterprise.

Edward I's campaigns in Scotland and Wales consumed wood at an alarming rate. For the building of the timber palisade of the peel at Lochmaben, Dumfriesshire (a relatively minor undertaking in the military campaign), nearly three acres of woodland were required, while 400 boards for roofing towers were also brought from Inglewood Forest. At the opposite end of the scale twelve oaks were needed to build a relatively humble home.

The result of this demand for wood was a serious threat to the natural environment. Britain was not densely forested in the Middle Ages (see p. 69) and by the thirteenth century timber was being imported, particularly from Scandinavia, to make up the dwindling local supply.

Medieval people were very conscious of the need for forest conservation. One of the solutions was coppicing, the planning of which was fully understood. Coppiced areas were protected from deer and other animals, sometimes even with earthworks.

In 1179 the Exchequer imposed a 'common and fixed penalty' for those making assarts in forest land – the process of claiming land by cutting back forest and then planting it. This penalty was fixed at a perpetual rent of one shilling for each acre sown with wheat, and 'expence [*sic*] for each sown with oats'.

Around 1100, Bishop Herbert de Losinga left detailed instructions for the preservation of woodland at Thorpe Wood near Norwich, and after 1257 the kings ceased to give gifts of timber.

Forest plantation was an idea introduced at the time of the Norman Conquest. Most of this was intended to provide hunting grounds for the king, and within the forests special laws prevailed. Some forests were used simply as sources of timber. Licences were granted for assarts in royal forests, and these followed inquests to determine how much wood might be felled without damaging the forest too badly. Normally the granting of a licence also required the construction of a hedge round the cleared area that would allow deer free passage but would keep out cattle, pigs or horses.

Due to the growing scarcity of timber in the later Middle Ages, other fuels were sought of which one was coal. Known in Roman Britain, it was of little consequence until the full Middle Ages, when it was increasingly used as a household fuel, and in a variety of industries – lime-burning, brewing, dying and iron working.

By the thirteenth century the main coal-fields of Britain seem to have been exploited – Newcastle, Nottinghamshire, Derbyshire, Shropshire and those in South Wales and Scotland. Sea coal was picked up on the shore in Northumberland and Durham, and was inferior to the pit coal that was mined.

Open-cast mining in shallow pits was the first method employed, but soon the Newcastle miners were running underground galleries which tended to cause subsidence. So extensive was the mining round the city that it was deemed too dangerous to go there at night, for fear of falling into open pits.

In 1278 a man was fined for digging a trench across a road in his search for the mineral. By the end of the thirteenth century the export trade was considerable, though as early as 1200 there are records of ships reaching Bruges with English coal.

Pollution   A side-effect of the coal industry was industrial pollution. Queen Eleanor, staying in Nottingham Castle in 1257, had to leave because of the fumes from the sea coal burned in the city.

In 1285 and 1288 there were serious complaints in London about infection and the contamination of the air caused by the burning of coal in limekilns. Following an enquiry, in 1307 a royal proclamation banned the use of sea coal in Southwark, Wapping and East Smithfield. It was largely ineffective, and by the time of Elizabeth I the problem was still acute. In 1578 the London Company of Brewers offered to burn wood instead of sea coal near the Palace of Westminster, since the queen 'findeth herselfe greatly greeved and anoyed with the taste and smoke of the sea-cooles' (Galloway, R. L. *A History of Coal Mining in Britain*, Newton Abbott, 1969, 24).

The iron industry not only polluted with its smoke, but also with noise. A medieval English poet noted,

> Swart smutted smiths, smattered with smoke,
> Drive me to death with din of their dints;
> Such noise on nights ne heard men never,
> What [with] knaven cry and clattering of knocks!
>
> (Quoted in Coulton, G. C. *Life in the Middle Ages* II,
> Cambridge, 1929, 99).

Rivers too, ran with the effluent of industry. Tanning and butchery were particularly antisocial in this respect. Tanning was so unpleasant, it had to be located on the edge of towns (to mimimize the fire risk) from Saxon times on.

In 1425 ale brewing was prompting complaints of water pollution since it was responsible for the 'impayring and corruption' of the river:

> Grevous compleynt [was made] that mochel people of the same ton brwen hure [their] ale and maken hure mete with water from the ryver of the said toun, the which said ryver ther ben certeyn persones dwellying upon, as Barbers [tanners] and White Tawyers, that leyen many diverse hides … impayring and corrupcion of the said water of the rever biforesaid, and in destruction of the ffyscvhe therynne to gret harmyng and noissaunce of the said people (*Victoria County History of Essex*, II (1907), 459).

This river pollution was notably caused by industrial chemicals, including alum, lime oil and tannic acids.

In 1388 at a meeting in Cambridge the English parliament passed the world's first national anti-pollution act. It stated that the

air … is greatly corrupt and infect and many maladies and other intolerable Diseases do daily happen.

This was attributed to pollution of land and water with rubbish, which had henceforth to be transported out of the towns. The citizens could complain to the Chancellor if they felt the civic authorities were not enforcing the law.

Science and Ideas

Against these practical developments, the medieval period was not as sterile of scientific development as is sometimes thought. It was however dominated by 'books of secrets' which were not repositories of arcane knowledge and magic, but essentially practical recipe books, collections of formulae, experiments and instruction manuals. They also contained medical prescriptions, cooking recipes, tricks and practical jokes.

They were based on the belief that nature was full of secret forces that could be manipulated by the application of basic rules and techniques, and used for personal profit or the good of mankind. They belonged to a tradition which went back to Aristotle, and laid the basis for experimental science in the Renaissance and later – largely through the dissemination of the 'secrets' by the development of printing in the later fifteenth and sixteenth centuries.

To the medieval mind there were two kinds of science: that which was available to many, and that which was revealed only to the few. This was an idea inherited from the Classical world.

Classical medicine was one area of ancient learning which survived more or less intact, but medieval medicine was practical and built on what had been learned before. In particular, medieval scholars learned the properties of plants unknown to Classical physicians.

Similarly, the medieval world inherited the Classical world's knowledge of glassmaking, metallurgy, ceramics, dyeing, and painting, and the period saw the proliferation of practical manuals to such crafts, though many garbled the original recipes.

Another area of medieval learning was derived from the Arab world – from the twelfth century it provided the West with books on occult science, astrology, alchemy, magic and divination.

The growth of medieval science is well exemplified by Roger Bacon, a Franciscan friar and philosopher (*c.*1220–1292) who read and translated an Arabic work known as the *Secret of Secrets*, which made him turn from philosophy to experimental science. He had a vision of a universal science, not for the masses (who would not understand it) but revealed by God to the patriarchs and prophets.

Roger Bacon was already anticipating the future with his ideas – indeed, he was mentioned by Leonardo da Vinci in one of his notebooks, and may have inspired him:

Machines of navigation can be constructed, without rowers ... Also a chariot can be constructed, that will move with incalculable speed without any draught animal ... Also flying machines may be constructed ... bridges over rivers without pillars or any supports ... (quoted in Jean Gimpel, *The Medieval Machine*, London, 1976, 146).

Of the other inventions suggested by Bacon, the diving helmet was pioneered by Konrad Keyser in Germany in the late fourteenth century.

Bacon produced detailed drawings of the eye, and experimented with lenses and parabolic mirrors. His mathematical calculations showed the errors of the Julian calendar (attributed to Julius Caesar and current in the Middle Ages), though his suggested alterations went unheeded and it was not until Pope Gregory XIII introduced the Gregorian calendar (used today) in 1582, that his suggestions were taken up.

Before Bacon there had been others, including his teacher, Robert Grosseteste (*c.*1175–1253), the first chancellor of Oxford University and the Bishop of Lincoln. Grosseteste too had worked on corrections to the calendar, and was also interested in optics, particularly magnification. He argued that mathematics were essential for an understanding of the physical world. He also considered that light was the creation of God out of autodiffusion, out of which He had created the dimensions of space and all living things.

Medicine

Medieval medicine reflected the contemporaneous approach to science, and the persistence of superstition.

For medieval people, death was an ever-present threat, and illness a commonplace occurrence from which medicine offered little relief. Plagues and famines were widespread, hygiene was poor and diet was bad from the highest ranks of society to the lowest.

War and childbirth took their tolls. It has been estimated from Continental evidence that women had a life expectancy of twenty-nine years and six months, men about a year less. This seems to have applied even to those who led comparatively sheltered lives – monks in Westminster Abbey, for example, could not realistically hope to survive much past thirty. In a closed community such as a monastery infectious diseases would have spread rapidly.

Medieval ideas about medicine stemmed from underlying concepts about the body which had been handed down from the Classical world and further elaborated upon by early Christian theologians. Diseases of the body and sins of the soul were seen as closely related. Illnesses were punishments visited upon people by God for their sins.

The fact that suffering on this earth would offset suffering in the hereafter was one way in which medieval people tried to come to terms with their afflictions. Madness in particular was seen by the Church to be the result of the patient's intensive pursuit of one of the seven deadly sins. Wrath, gluttony or sexual vice were deemed particularly likely to induce insanity since they increased the heat of the body, while sloth cooled it too much, leading to listlessness and stupor.

Demons too could cause madness, as could the forces of the planets. The moon gave its name to lunacy.

Leprosy, which was particularly prevalent in the earlier Middle Ages, was believed to be sexually transmitted, and due to an excess of lechery; intercourse between a man and a menstruating woman, for example,

Female leper, from a 15c Franciscan Missal, English, British Library Lansdowne MS Douce 313, f. 394 v (Jenny Laing)

159

would very probably produce a leprous child. Heretics were spiritual lepers, and both were classed with Jews and homosexuals as people who had sunk into an inescapable mire of sin.

Prayer, penance and pilgrimage were all methods of seeking relief from disease (see p. 96).

From the Classical world the medieval people acquired the concept of the body as a part of the universe, working in the same way as the larger whole. The universe was composed of four elements: fire, water, earth and air. Thus the human body depended on the balance of four humours: choler or yellow bile (the fire humour); phlegm (the water humour); black bile (the earth humour) and blood (air).

These had to be carefully balanced, for if one became dominant, the 'complexion' of the afflicted was altered. A surfeit of choler produced a choleric personality; phlegm a phlegmatic; black bile a melancholic and blood a sanguine. Women were deemed colder and wetter than men and thus more often phlegmatic.

Astrology Astrology also played an important part in later medieval medicine. Each of the houses of the zodiac and the planets affected the health of those born under them. Those born with Saturn in the ascendant would be melancholic and swarthy, prone to skin diseases and dirty in their habits. If born under the moon they would be indecisive worriers, prone to colds and insanity.

From the third century AD onwards, the Church had consigned astrologers to a pit of disapproval which also contained prostitutes, pimps and gladiators. By the late medieval period, especially after the Black Death (which was seen to have spread due to astrological factors), astrology became popular as a guide to treatment. Since illnesses were seen to reach a crisis point, after which the patient recovered or died, the day and time of the crisis point were seen to influence the outcome.

The occult arts could also be used to cause illnesses. Alice Perrers, the mistress of Edward III, was believed to have used magic to trap the King. This she had done by obtaining from a Dominican friar wax effigies of herself and the king, herbs and spells devised by the Egyptian necromancer Nectanebus and a ring which had belonged to Moses.

The wicked friar was trapped by two shire knights posing as patients who went to him with bottles of urine and tempted him to treat them by offering a fee he could not refuse.

Alchemy Alchemy was not far removed in its principles from medieval medicine, since such techniques as distillation were needed for both, and it involved the idea of reducing the four elements to one; the 'quintessence'. In Scotland the House of Stuart was particularly susceptible to the occult arts. James IV set up the French alchemist and physician John Damian in a laboratory, setting him the task of discovering the philosopher's stone, which turned base metal into gold.

he causet the King believe that he, be multiplyinge and utheris his inventions, wold make fine golde of uther metall, quhilk science he callit the quintassence; qhhairupon the King maid greit cost, bot all in vaine.

In a further mission impossible,

This Abbott tuk in hand to flie with wingis, and to ... that effect he causet mak ane pair of wingis of fedderis, quhilkis beand fessinit apoun him.

Undaunted by any misgivings he 'flew of the castell wall of Stiverling'. Hardly surprisingly it is then recorded that 'bot shortlie he fell to the ground and brak his thee bane'. (Quoted in J. D. Comrie, *History of Scottish Medicine*, London, 1932, 154).

Roger Bacon was of the view that health could be assured 'bi power of astronomye, alkamye and prospectief and of sciences experimental'.

Medieval Doctors

It was within these intellectual and spiritual frames of reference that medieval medical practitioners worked. Where there was a build-up of any one humour, it could be disposed of in the healthy individual in sweat, tears, urine or faeces. Sneezing could clear the head. When the natural system for maintaining the balance broke down, illness resulted.

Medieval doctors stressed that prevention was better than cure, and accordingly advocated a healthy lifestyle, in which diet, exercise and a reduction in stress figured prominently. A thirteenth-century doctor, Bernard Gordon, who practised at Montpellier, encouraged checking a patient's home to see if it was afflicted by noisy neighbours or was in an area where barking dogs, drunks or bandits might cause stress and thus further disease.

Certain foods were deemed suitable for specific imbalances of the humours – warm and moist foods such as chicken and blancmange were considered 'temperate' and therefore conducive to a good humoral state.

Successful medicine depended on the skilful interpretation of symptoms; different humoral imbalances could produce similar diseases in different types of people.

One of the best diagnostic aids was uroscopy, and urine samples were contemplated in jordans (medieval chamber pots) to determine from their colour the best treatment of the patient. The basic skills were learned from coloured charts (of limited value given the range of pigments available) and samples were taken regularly to check on progress. Diagnostic practices such as taking the pulse or examining blood or faecal samples were also in use.

Having determined the cause of the problem, treatment involved such diversions as laxatives, diuretics, cautery, fumigation, hot baths and cupping. Herbal remedies, too, played their part.

If in doubt, doctors tended to order enemas (clysters). John of Ardene swore by a simple concoction of water, mallows, green camomile, wheat bran, salt, honey, various herbs and soap, pumped

Prognostication and geomantic figures, from chart made for Richard II in 1391, Bodley 581, f. 20v (Bodleian Library)

OPPOSITE: *Malign conjunction between Saturn & Jupiter, late 15C English MS Rawl. B214, f. 197v (Bodleian Library)*

OPPOSITE: *Diagram of man showing veins, from the late 15C. Book of the Barber Surgeons of York, Egerton MS 2572, f. 50r (British Library)*

OVERLEAF: *Mummers wearing masks, MS 264, f. 21v (Bodleian Library)*

into the patient by way of a greased pipe connected to a clyster bag, while the patient rubbed his abdomen with his hand.

In the fourteenth century, acute lethargy and 'confusion of reason' might be treated in the following dramatic way. People should talk loudly to lethargics and 'tie their extremities lightly and rub their palms and soles hard'. Their feet should be put in salt water up to the middle of their shins, but more alarmingly, the practitioner should 'pull their hair and nose, and squeeze their toes and fingers tightly, and cause pigs to squeal in their ears'.

Predictably it was necessary to,

give a sharp clyster at the beginning ... and open the vein of the head, or nose, or forehead, and draw blood from the nose with the bristles of a boar.

If this did not work, it was suggested that one should,

put a feather, or straw, in his nose to compel him to sneeze, and do not ever desist from hindering him from sleeping; and let human hair or other evil-smelling thing be burned under his nose. Apply, moreover, the cupping horn between the shoulders, and let a feather be put down his throat, to cause vomitting, and shave the back of his head, and rub oil of roses and vinegar and wild celery juice thereon ...

(*Rosa Anglica, sev Rosa Medicinae Johannis Anglici*, Irish Texts Society, vol. XXXV, ed. W. Wulff, 1929, 231–3).

Blood-letting was a popular cure, although if carried out with excessive zeal it could lead to death. In 1278, jurors at an inquest in London were informed that a skinner called William le Paumer had died in West Cheap as a result of badly-performed blood-letting. It was held to be an accident.

There were many different points for blood-letting on the body, each connected with different ailments. The two veins in the 'nek hole' were to be tapped in the case of leprosy or 'straytness of wind'. The favourite letting point was in the basilic vein, just below the elbow, which was deemed to clear the liver and spleen of impurities.

The medical properties of herbs were controlled by the manner of their collection, and by whom they were collected. Betony had to be picked in August by a small child 'or the sonn ryse', while marigold was to be gathered when the moon had entered the house of Virgo. The herbalist had also to recite the appropriate prayers while at work.

If all else failed, the charms and incantations were used to ease chilbirth, cure impotence and frigidity, effect contraception, staunch blood, cure toothache, remove boils, banish ringworm and even heal broken limbs.

Surgery Physicians dealt with the inside of the body, surgeons with the outside. The latter were skilled with their hands, and saw themselves as carpenters of the body. They were originally butchers – hence modern surgeons are referred to as Mr not Dr – and their task was to rid the body of superfluous humours by physically cutting them out.

Lead plague crosses, London (Jenny Laing)

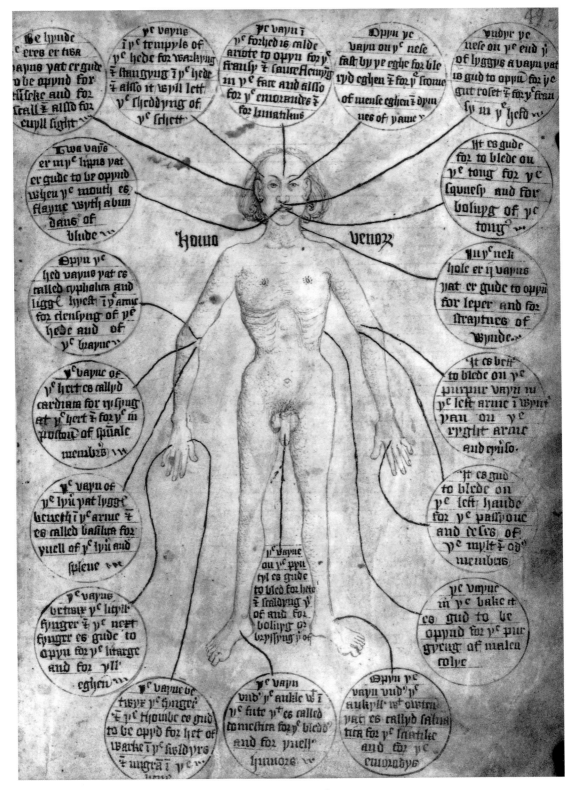

re tyr le telkeduret
ust a alixandre .

Surgery was usually a last resort, but one which had been successful in the case of breast cancer, fistulae, haemorrhoids, gangrene and scrofula.

Medieval illustrations of surgery give no indication of the pain suffered by the victims. As it was, many of the preparations for relieving pain or inducing sleep were potentially lethal. One concoction called 'dwale' consisted of gall from a sow or castrated boar, lettuce, briony, opium, henbane and hemlock juice mixed with wine. The alcohol, hemlock and opium would have rendered the patient incapable, and the henbane and briony would have speeded up the passage of the poisons out of the body. Hemlock was tricky because too much was rapidly fatal.

Medical ethics   In the case of surgery, medical ethics could be a problem. Around 1206 Robert Courson in a discussion of penance considered medical ethics and culpability, and pronounced that while surgeons were obliged to offer cures which had some hope of success, they ought not to try anything that was dangerous, especially not for the fees they might thereby obtain.

Apothecaries

The advent of the apothecary (forerunner of the chemist and pharmacist) was an important development of the Middle Ages. Of all the medicaments dispensed by apothecaries, none was of greater esteem than that which was called 'treacle' – theriac, the medieval cure-all.

Among its supposed uses were the cure of fevers, the prevention of internal swellings, the unblocking of internal stoppages, clearing the skin of blemishes, the alleviation of heart trouble, dropsy, epilepsy and palsy, the induction of sleep, the improvement of the digestion, the strengthening of limbs, the healing of wounds, the means of inducing vaginal bleeding for curing a prolapsed uterus, and as a cure for the plague. It was also handy as a remedy for snake bites.

Specialist treacle dealers could be found in major cities. Treacle was imported from the Continent, where it was made under licence. It was a complex formula, and a recipe developed by the ancient Greek physician Galen involved some sixty-four ingredients, including the flesh of skinned and roasted vipers. In the Middle Ages 'Galene' as it was called took forty days to make and up to twelve years to mature.

Theriac was known to the Arabs, whose learning on the subject also passed to the West. The techniques used in its production were difficult and could even prove fatal, so there was careful regulation. It was imported from Italy by the Grocers' Company, who were responsible for the quality – its cost meant that inferior theriac ('fals treacle') was often sold.

There was much trouble with bad (therapeutic) drugs in the Middle Ages. Opium was mixed with barley flour, ambergris with salt, and camphor with powdered marble, in attempts to make a quick profit.

Apothecaries became a by-word for sharp practice and dishonest trading.

Successful apothecaries, honest as well as dishonest, could expect to earn good money, and none more than those employed by royalty; a subsidiary part of that job involved fumigating the royal bedding and clothes, before perfuming them.

Witchcraft

Despite the scientific advances and the strength of the Church, medieval people were highly superstitious.

Witchcraft is a phenomenon of long duration in Europe, but prior to the later medieval period was relatively unimportant in Britain. While the age of witch-hunts did not come until the sixteenth and more particularly the seventeenth century, the belief grew in the later Middle Ages, when cults flourished in a time of spiritual uncertainty. It was essentially a heresy, but was not deemed significant enough to be banned as such until a Bull of Pope Innocent VIII in 1484. It did not become a capital offence in Britain until 1542.

Eleanor Cobham, wife of the Duke of Gloucester, was brought to trial for witchcraft in 1441, accused of conspiring with her secretary, Roger Bolingbroke (an Oxford scholar), and a distinguished physician Thomas Southwell. It was claimed that they had used the black arts to try to establish when Henry VI would die. To that end it was alleged that she had invoked evil spirits and demons and used magical figures, vestments, and a book of necromancers' oaths and experiments. Necromancy was particularly popular during this period.

Although magic was a component of most medical practice, it was particularly associated with women, who could be either village 'wise-women' or witches, versed in both black and white witchcraft, as the occasion dictated. Herbal preparations were a part of their stock-in-trade, some of them remedies, some simply magical concoctions.

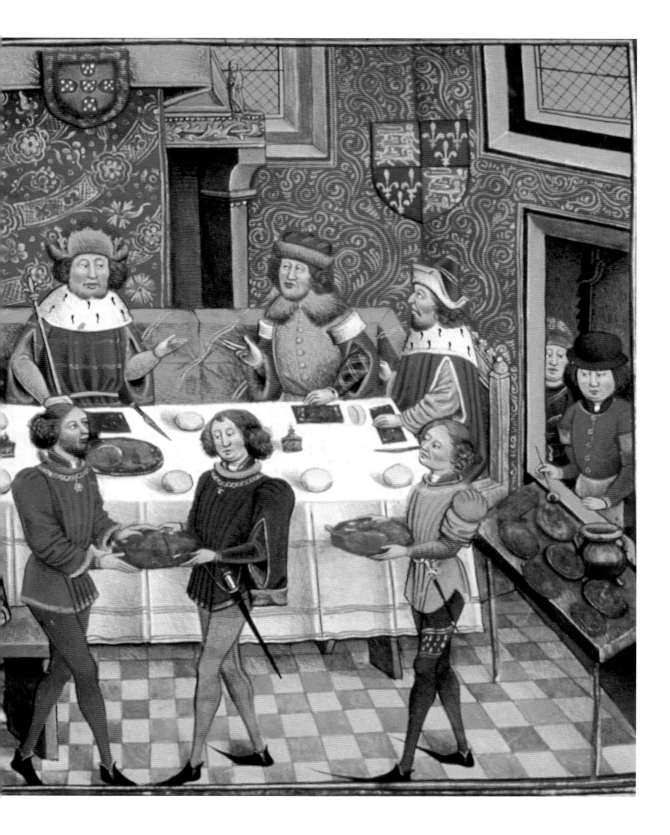

RIGHT: *Kaimes Brooch, Midlothian.
Gold, c.1300 (National Museums of
Scotland)*

*15C Gold hook fastener, with part
of leather belt, Thames foreshore
(Lloyd Laing)*

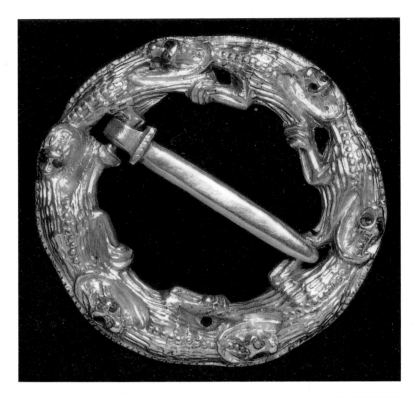

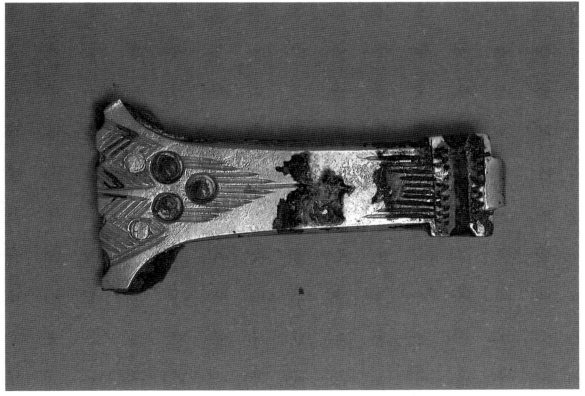

8 · Leisure and fashion

EVEN APPARENTLY INNOCUOUS leisure pursuits could be dangerous in the Middle Ages. Juliana Cordwaner was stabbed to death in the mid thirteenth century because her male chess opponent did not like the idea of her winning. The romance of Fulk Fitzwarine records how the future King John lost his temper at chess and tried to brain his opponent with the board. Although William Caxton produced a serious manual for aspiring grand masters – *Game and Playe of Chesse*, published in the 1470s, the game clearly excited strong emotions.

Games

Cards were introduced in the fifteenth century, having originated in Muslim India. Although no medieval playing cards survive, the queen depicted on modern cards is Elizabeth of York, daughter of Edward IV and wife of Henry VII.

Among board games may be singled out merrills (merelles). This had a board with nine holes, and it was played like noughts-and-crosses – the aim was to get three pieces in a row. Boards for the game have even been found on the benches of the cloisters of Westminster Abbey and Canterbury Cathedral. The game was elaborated into a game with nine pieces for each player instead of three, and was known as nine-mens morris or larger merrills. This game became more complicated still, with more pieces and more complex rules – in the form of Fox and Geese, the fox captured geese by jumping over them, and the geese tried to corner the fox so that he could not move. Edward IV enjoyed playing it.

A game called tables was the equivalent of modern backgammon. A pit at Commercial Road, Gloucester, yielded a more or less intact board and a set of thirty pieces, dating from the eleventh century. All that was missing was the dice. The pieces were richly decorated with a variety of subjects.

Stone boards have survived from medieval contexts, such as Melrose Abbey. Chess pieces have survived in some numbers, ranging from the beautifully and intricately carved twelfth-century Norse Lewis chessmen, to simpler pieces such as the jet example from Warrington or the bone examples from Dorchester, Dorset.

The Halmote Rolls of Durham documented that in 1366 all householders were directed to 'chastise their servants who had been accustomed to play at dice'.

If this type of game was too sedentary, there were other ways of passing the time. In 1282 an English parish priest decided to widen the

Chessman, ivory, mid 13th century (Ashmolean Museum, Oxford)

Oxwich brooch,
Glamorgan, 1320–1440,
cameos perhaps c.1250
(National Museum of
Wales)

BELOW: *Dunstable swan
jewel, gold and enamel,
c.1400 (British Museum)*

RIGHT: *Courtly dancing,
Douce MS 195, f. 7
(Bodleian Library)*

174

Classical education of the maidens in his parish by holding a celebration in honour of Bacchus – he danced, sang and carried models of human reproductive organs attached to a pole.

Feast-day games   Hocktide could be equally diverting. On the second Tuesday after Easter the village men challenged the women and each sex tried to capture the other, those caught having to pay a forfeit. In the late thirteenth century the ladies of the court managed to capture Edward I, and forced him into bed to pay his forfeit, the precise nature of which is not recorded.

On St Valentine's Day people played 'Lady Anne' which was a guessing game, at the end of which they paired off and went to play games *à deux* somewhere else. There was traditional food on this day – peacock eggs, pomegranates and cakes painted red and blue.

The Midsummer Solstice (June 23), which was also the Feast of the Eve of St John, was marked by feasting, drinking, playing sexy games, building bonfires, carrying torches and rolling burning wheels down hillsides. Londoners decorated their houses with garlands, and everywhere was lit up, especially by bonfires.

Midsummer was also thought to be a good time for predicting the future – girls used to pull petals off flowers saying, in time-honoured way, 'He loves me, he loves me not'.

Christmas celebrations have in many cases a familiar sound to them. The cutting of mistletoe seems to have been a pagan Celtic survival, and the yule log was derived from pagan winter solstice events. Carols were sung, including 'The Twelve Days of Christmas' and 'Good Christian Men Rejoice', and there were wassails, feasts, gift giving, and mummers (dancers).

Christmas was the time for the Lord of Misrule, one of the lowly members of the manor who was allowed to be lord for a day and order feasts and entertainments for his fellow riff-raff. It was an echo of the Saturnalia that attended Roman mid-winter celebrations, in which slaves were masters for a day, and the masters slaves.

A variant was the Feast of Fools or the Feast of the Ass, when subdeacons were elevated in ecclesiastical status for the day, and clerics dressed up in masks or costumes, danced lewd jigs and sang rude songs with the appropriate gestures. Nuns though more decorous held similar events, with an abbess appointed for the day. A further such tradition was the Boy Bishop festival, particularly a feature of Bury St Edmunds. A boy was appointed bishop for a day and lead tokens were issued in his honour. These he distributed to the poor in a type of Maundy ceremony.

St Swithun's Day was an occasion on which to mark the richness of the harvest. There was bobbing for apples, races, currant bread and plums. On Lammas Day in August there were candelit processions, and bread was ceremonially saved for the next year. Halloween was little different in the Middle Ages from now. Children put on masks and pretended to be wandering souls – if they were not rewarded with soul cakes they were allowed to play tricks on their victims.

Many of these celebrations were a survival from a remote pagan past, so the Church did its best to discourage them, but sepulchre rites and resurrection plays did not have quite the same appeal.

Sports   Tennis could be surprisingly hazardous – one of the ancestors of John Hampden lost three manors for hitting the Black Prince with his racquet. Football could be lethal in unexpected ways. One lay player collided with a canon, William de Spalding, and impaled himself on a sheathed knife the cleric was carrying. He died six days later.

This was also a problem at Caunton, Notts, where in the time of Henry VI one William Bartram,

being struck in his most sensitive parts by the foot of one who played with him, sustained long and intolerable pains; but, having seen in a dream the glorious king Henry, suddenly received the benefit of health. (*Miracles of King Henry VI*, ed. Knox R. & Lesley, S. 1923, 131).

The same account also has a gloss on football:

young men, in country sport, propel a huge ball not by throwing it into the air but by striking and rolling it along the ground, and that not with their hands but with their feet. A game, I say ... more common undignified and worthless than any other kind of game, rarely ending but with some loss, accident, or disadvantage to the players themselves.

Among other pastimes, mention should be made of archery, blind man's buff, bowling, dice, hammer throwing, hockey, morris-dancing, quarter-staff contests, quoits, shuttlecock, skittles, tennis, wrestling, swimming, hunting and jousting (see p. oo).

Musical Entertainment

Music was an important element in medieval life. Instruments included violins, drums, harps, lutes, organs, citoles, psalteries, flutes and horns (see pp. 198–199). More exotic instruments were used, such as the bagpipes shown played by an animal in the fifteenth century Rosslyn Chapel in Midlothian.

In 1350 Edward III employed five trumpeters, 1 citole player, 5 pipers, 1 tabouret player (a type of drum), 1 naker player (a type of drum), 2 clarion blowers and 1 fiddler.

Minstrels and jugglers were often to be found in bands of travelling players. These sometimes included women, but *jongleuses* were deemed to be lower class, and often equated, erroneously, with prostitutes. In 1306 several women were amongst the minstrels employed at the knighthood ceremony for Edward (later II). One used the stage name of Pearl in the Egg. The Treasury also paid around this time an aptly named Maud Makejoy to entertain King Edward with dancing and acrobatics.

Magnates usually had their own entertainers – musicians, jugglers and dwarves.

Two 14c musicians (Joan Nunn)

Theatrical Performances

These were also popular and originated in ecclesiastical efforts to instruct the masses in Biblical stories. In the eleventh century they

Gittern, early 14th century (British Museum)

were performed in churches, but as time progressed they were moved out into churchyards and involved complex scenery, costumes and even special effects, sometimes operated by machinery. Lay involvement was a feature of these plays, which were in the vernacular, with musicians performing offstage.

The subject matter remained primarily moralistic – saints' lives, Bible stories and, later on, morality plays with personifications of virtues and vices. Women were not normally permitted to perform, however, though there are some instances recorded, such as a four-teenth-century abbess of Barking, who put on an Easter play with her nuns wearing costumes she made herself.

Some of the medieval cycles of plays still survive, such as the Chester Mystery Plays, along with such moralistic plays as the story of *Every-man.*

Despite the high moral tone of the subject matter of plays, some clerics did not approve. The bishop of Salisbury, Thomas de Cobham (d.1313) categorized and condemned actors thus:

There are three kinds of play-actors. Some transform and transfigure their own bodies by base contortions and base gestures, or by basely denuding themselves, or by wearing horrible masks; and all such are to be damned unless they abandon their calling.

He had a low opinion of them:

Others again, do no work, but commit criminal deeds, having no fixed abode, but haunting the courts of great men and backbiting the absent opprobiously and ignominiously in order to please others. Such men are also to be damned …

He continued:

There is also a third kind of actors who have musical instruments for men's delight; and as such are of two kinds. Some haunt public drinkings and wanton assemblies, where they sing divers songs to move men to wantoness; and such are to be damned like the rest.

Although he admitted that some who 'sing the deeds of princes and the lives of the saints', could be tolerated, in general he considered that,

all commit mortal sin who give any of their goods to buffoons or jesters or the aforesaid play-actors; for to give to play-actors is no other than to throw our money away.

Food and Feasts

Of all the entertainments available in medieval Britain, eating had universal appeal. Sumptuous feasts were available only to the rich, and most of the existing menus and recipes were for their delectation alone. But although their repasts were more modest, even the comparatively humble marked festivals with special gastronomic delights.

To modern stomachs medieval recipes often appear totally repellent, and certainly would have been extremely strong tasting and spicy. It is difficult to recreate medieval recipes adequately because the quantities of the ingredients are not specified.

Cormorant, whale, seal and porpoise were considered delicacies, but failing those, people could tuck in to tasty vulture or heron. Sugared oysters were quite acceptable too.

Sugar was regarded as a spice, and being rare and exotic could be put with anything. It was imported from Syria, Rhodes, Cyprus, Crete, Alexandria and Sicily. In the late fifteenth century ordinary quality sugar retailed at prices up to 3 shillings, which, given that geese cost 3 to 4 pence and peacocks were 12 pence each, was a substantial outlay. One recipe suggests, with a typically casual panache and lack of precision baffling to modern cooks:

Take brawn and cut it thin. Then take the yolks of eggs and some of the white therewith. Then take manches flour and draw the eggs through a strainer. Then take a good quantity of sugar, saffron, and salt.

The recipe then felt it necessary to stipulate that a, 'fair [clean] pan with French grease,' should be set over the fire.

The dish could then be completed:

When the grease is hot, take the brawn and put in batter and turn it well therein, and then put it in the pan with the grease, and let [them] fry together a little while. Then take it up into a fair dish, and cast sugar thereon, and serve forth (*Two Fifteenth Century Cookery Books*, ed Austin, T. 1883, 43).

English cookery in the middle ages was based on the French, and there were three basic rules: never do anything simply, keep adding the spices and totally obscure the original flavour. Thus a recipe for poached eggs specified,

Take eggs, break them, and seethe them in hot water. Then take them up as whole thou mayest. Then take flour and mix with milk and cast thereto sugar or honey and a little powdered ginger, and boil all together, and colour with saffron. And lay the eggs in dishes and cast the broth above, and cast on powder enough. Blanche powder is best. (*Two Fifteenth Century Cookery Books*, 24).

Blanche powder was made from ginger, cinnamon and nutmegs.

Spices were employed in quantity partly because they were exotic and costly. They came from the Far East, along the caravan route, and were traded to Alexandria and Aleppo among other places, where they were bought by Venetians and Genoese for trading on to France and England. Richard de Swinfield (1289–90) has left for us records of some of his household expenses, which included 'cloves, cubebs, mace, saffron, sugar, garingale [galingale, from cypress root], cinnamon, ginger, raw and preserved pepper, cummin, coriander, liquorice, buckwheat, aniseed, and gromil.' Spices were seen to aid digestion, and to obscure the fact that the meat was often 'high'.

In one year spice and pepper cost Sir Thomas Cawarden £10, the same amount that he spent on wine (Rhenish, red, white, sack, claret and malmsey).

Sharp tasting juices (sometimes fermented, sometimes not) were also used in cookery. The juice of crab apples, green grapes and gooseberries was poured on meat, fish and eggs. Verjuice was sometimes made from fermented grape juice, to which salt was added.

Sauces and colouring agents also figure in recipes, and almonds in one form or another were of major importance. They were boiled, stamped, sugared, blanched, ground, mixed with ale and water, strained, flavoured with saffron, sugar and salt. Almond milk, almond butter and fried cream of almonds all make their appearance. In the 258 recipes given in *Two Fifteenth Century Recipe Books*, eighty-three required almonds.

The names of particular dishes are often misleading to modern readers. 'Blancmange' was a meat or fish dish made with sweetened almond milk to which sugar and salt were added. A decent 'custard' was made with veal, herbs, pepper, cinnamon, cloves, mace, saffron, wine, ginger and, as if an afterthought, eggs. One item that did not have ginger in it was 'gingerbread'.

Pies were popular, the pastry crust being termed, perhaps with macabre humour, a 'coffin'. Venison and hare were often put into them. Hedgehogs – yrchouns (urchins) – too could be a tasty delicacy. Other creatures of the feast table were cranes, bitterns, curlews, quails, snipe, plover, woodcocks, fieldfares, teal, and gulls.

However not all 'dieticians' were in favour of some of these:

A crane is harde of dygestyon and doth ingender evyll blode … Olde pecockes be harde of dygestyon … Al maner of smale Byrdes be good

and lyght of dygestyon, excepte sparrowes, whiche be hard of dygestyon.
(Andrew Boorde, *Dyetary*, 1542).

Great feasts   Detailed accounts survive of some of the great feasts given in medieval England. One of the most fully documented was that given on the occasion of the marriage of Margaret, daughter of Henry III, to Alexander III of Scotland, which was held in York on 26th December, 1251.

Preparations were put in hand by the summer. About 25,000 gallons of wine were ordered well in advance (in August). Some 300 red and fallow deer were ordered to be caught, slaughtered and salted. In October a requisition went out for more meat – hens, game birds, rabbits, hares, pigs and boars.

In terms of quantity, the 7,000 hens seem to have been adequate, but another 100 boars and a further 1000 deer were ordered in November. Orders for the bread went out locally in the same month – 68,500 loaves costing £7,000 – closely followed by the rice, almonds and sugar list.

The fish order was left until December, when 60,000 herring, 1,000 greenfish (probably unsalted cod), 10,000 haddock and 500 conger eels were deemed essential. Freshwater fish were stored live until needed.

Feasts normally consisted of three or four courses (sometimes more) consisting of several dishes. That held by Richard III in 1483 on his coronation was a more extensive affair, with three courses of fifteen, sixteen and seventeen dishes.

The first course comprised five meat dishes, five bird dishes, one fish and four indeterminate dishes. The second course had four meat, six bird and probably two fish dishes, with the rest indeterminate. Nobody ate the third course as it was too dark by then for the guests to see what they were eating – they were given instead wafers (which could be meat or fish based) and hippocras (a mixture of red or white wine with in some cases, cinnamon, ginger, spikenard, galingale, cloves, long pepper, nutmeg, marjoram and cardamon, together with grains of paradise and flour of cinnamon, strained through bags). Although no record is made of it, the feast would have ended with 'ordynance' of wafers, fruit and spiced wine.

There were strict rules about who was to be served which dish. Top table was offered the entire menu, which included such delicacies as egrets (only thirty-six were served), while 'lordes and ladyes' were given a selection from two courses (with some dishes not offered to top table). The ordinary people had one course of three dishes.

The whole feast started with soup of a type called 'frumentie', made from boiled, hulled wheat and milk of almonds, which formed a stock to which in this case venison and spices were added.

Vegetables do not figure prominently – although eaten by all social orders, they were generally regarded as food for the lower classes. They included turnips or parsnips in pottage, onions, leeks, beans, radishes and carrots. Salads were rare, though John Howard, Duke of Norfolk, in 1482 bought 'erbes for a selad'.

At the end of each course a 'subtlety' was presented. This would be an ornament of some kind, often chosen to accord with a theme: for example, symbols of the seasons as the ages of man, or biblical subjects. Some were edible, of sugar or marzipan, others were probably purely decorative. Usually they were accompanied by an explanation, sometimes in verse. In less grand feasts the subtleties could be simpler, and did not always follow a theme.

Trumpets signalled the arrival of a course, and music was played during the feasting, as well as performances being given by dancers, acrobats and others.

Table manners   Medieval people were guided in table manners by the *Boke of Cutasye*, a fifteenth-century manual of etiquette. Many of the fundamental rules survived to be included in the Elizabethan *Boke of Nature* or *Schoole of Good Maners*, published in 1577, and, given the basic rules of hygiene, it is not surprising that many still hold today.

It was deemed necessary to advise,

Burnish no bones with thy teeth, for that is unseemly ... Belch thou near no man's face with a corrupt fumosity... Blow not your nose on the napkin where you should wipe your hand; but cleanse it in your handkerchief ...

However four centuries have brought some changes from 'If thou must spit, or blow thy nose ... let it not lie upon the ground, but tread though it out right', whereas 'blow not thy nose, nor look thereon; to most men it is loath', still seems reasonable.

The book continues with the eminently sensible advice,

Blow not thy pottage nor drink, for it is not commendable; for if thou be not whole of thy body, thy breath is corruptable. Scratch not thy head, nor put thou not thy finger in thy mouth.

Trying to keep these rules in mind, good mannered guests had other skills to master, most of which are negatives – and only too familiar to modern parents. People should not, for example, spit on or over the table, or scratch the dog. Picking the teeth with a knife, drinking with the mouth full of food, telling unseemly stories and wiping the teeth or eyes with the tablecloth were frowned upon. Polite guests did not lean on their elbows, dip their thumbs in drink, nor their food into the common salt cellar. They made no noise in supping pottage and did not leave finger marks on the tablecloth.

Well mannered guests put their trenchers in front of them and waited until food was brought from the kitchen. They had a duty to ensure their nails were clean.

One difference not applicable today was the exhortation that a person should not bite his (or her) bread and put it down – sufficient only for immediate needs was to be broken off and the rest left for the poor people.

Bread had to be broken correctly: the loaf was pared to remove the crust, then broken in two, from bottom to top. The top crust was then divided into four parts, and the bottom into three. The serving of food was attended by elaborate ceremony, and preceded by the washing of hands (very necessary since much eating was done with the fingers dipped into communal dishes). The water was sometimes perfumed with rose leaves, thyme, lavender, sage, camomile, marjoram or orange peel, or a combination of these.

Hand-washing was done in accordance with a strict hierarchy, the towel and ewer being offered first to the most elevated. The guests took their seats in sequence according to rank. An Elizabethan *Booke of Precedence* probably reflects a long-established tradition when it advises that,

A Barron must go after his Creation, so that the Eldest barron goe uppermost; and the barronesse his wife must goe according to the same; … And a barron may have the Cover of his cupp holden underneath when he drinketh … a Baronesse may have no trayne borne; but having a gowne with a trayne, she ought to beare it herself.

Fashion

Fashionable clothing was a preoccupation of the rich during the Middle Ages, undergoing considerable change throughout the period, and varying according to rank. The apparel of the middle and lower social orders tended towards the practical, tunics being the norm.

The Norman Conquest saw increasing elaboration in male dress among the nobility, with the increased use of fur-lined cloaks and the wearing of both under- and over-tunics. Sleeves became long, as did hair and beards. Rich Norman women of fashion had tight gowns with long sleeves which hung down from the wrists and were sometimes knotted. They also had long trailing skirts and silk-broidered hair.

By the thirteenth century noblemen were wearing an under-tunic, a short upper tunic, a gown, hood and mantle, short boots with long toes and gloves. A hood, or a white coif was tied under the chin as standard. Ladies in the same period wore a tight-fitting gown, upper tunic and mantle. Married ladies and nuns wore a wimple (covering the forehead) or gorget (covering the throat and neck), and their hair was usually contained in a caul or net, covered with a veil. The origin of the wimple lay in the Mohammedan veil encountered by Crusaders.

Imported cloth of exotic origin became sought-after in the High Middle Ages. A rare surviving piece of weft-face compound silk twill survives from Southampton. Probably from Byzantium, this was apparently decorated with a formal plant motif. Another piece of silk from the same city was not unlike the turquoise blue facing of the cloak of an English bishop buried in 1372 in Nubia.

At the end of the thirteenth century new fashions spread from France, and were taken up by Piers Gaveston, a friend of Edward II, and other courtiers.

Fashion became increasingly elaborate in the time of Richard II, whose wife Anne of Bohemia introduced very pointed shoes, the points of which grew longer and longer until around 1410. They had gained popularity after the many Poles in her retinue who introduced the

13c women's dress, showing wimple (Jenny Laing)

style. In England they were known as 'crackowes' (after Cracow) or 'poulaines' (after Poland).

Richard introduced two new fashions to courtly circles as well — blowing the nose on a handkerchief, and eating with a fork.

15c shoe sole (Lloyd Laing)

By the time of Edward III noblemen were wearing short, tight-fitting embroidered coats, buttoned down the front, with sleeves buttoned from elbow to wrist and decorated with pendants called tippets, from the shoulder. A mantle was flung over the left shoulder, or failing that, a hood called a capuchon was worn, that had a streamer behind, called a liripipe. Edward tried to restrict the points on shoes by law — specifying that

No knight under the estate of a lord, esquire or gentleman, nor any other person, shall wear any shoes or boots having spikes or points exceeding the length of two inches, under the forfeiture of forty pence.

Late medieval leather mitten, Caerlaverock (Historic Scotland)

Women too were wearing long, tight-sleeved gowns, also with pendants from the upper arm, often decorated with armorial designs, as well as the open-sided over-dress known as the *cote-hardi*. This came in for adverse criticism from the churchmen of the day, one of whom, John Bromyard, wrote:

Christ opened his side for the redemption and salvation of many, and these others open their sides for lascivious and carnal provocation, and for the perdition of those who behold them.

John Waldeby was similarly forthright on the wearing of close-fitting garments and make-up:

If a noble painter, in the execution of some figure sculptures it well and artistically and also puts suitable colours upon it, would not the pupil or the owner of the figure do insult to such an artist, if he altered the form and colour of that same figure? So when women set about adorning their own persons by constricting themselves in tight clothing they wish to appear slender, and with artificial colours they desire to seem beautiful, thereby expressly insulting their Creator.

The ideal of female beauty seems to have been narrow shoulders and hips, rounded breasts, 'long smal armys' (long slim arms) and

14C fashions (Jenny Laing)

Wooden comb with inscription, Caerlaverock (Historic Scotland)

15C fashions (Jenny Laing)

Examples of 15c headdresses
(Joan Nunn)

graceful hands. Facial features had to be small and regular, and particularly admired was a small nose.

Female hairstyles were elaborate, often braided with gold network. The wimple however was going out of fashion in the fourteenth century, and during the fifteenth all manner of elaborate hairstyles and headgear came into fashion for women. Among these may be singled out an arrangement of wire frame with a kerchief over it made to look like square wings – the 'butterfly headdress', fashionable from around 1470 to 1490. Also popular were heart-shaped headdresses and Italian turbans, worn in the time of Henry VI, and tall steeple caps, popular in the time of Edward IV.

Jewellery

Jewellery in the Middle Ages was as sumptuous as it had been in previous centuries. The sparkle notable in modern cut stones however was lacking until the fifteenth century, when cutting was invented. Diamonds made their appearance in western Europe in the fourteenth century, and cabochon settings of rubies were also popular. Sapphires were believed to have magical powers. Jewellery could be made of almost anything, from gold and silver to pewter and tin.

The main item worn from the twelfth century onwards was the ring brooch. This was simply a ring, sometimes engraved or richly decorated with stone settings or mouldings, with a loose pin. Tiny examples were probably worn as functional fastenings where they would not be seen, elaborate examples were for adornment, as well as for fastening clothing at the neck. Of the many surviving examples the Oxwich Brooch with its re-used older cameos in beaded settings is exceptional, and dates from the fourteenth century. The Kaimes Brooch from Scotland is of gold, and is decorated with a series of animals chasing one another. Some brooches had inscriptions – one set with rubies and sapphires has an inscription in French on the back IO SUI ICI EN LIU DAMI: AMO ('I am here in place of a friend: love'), and Chaucer describes his prioress as wearing a brooch with the inscription, singularly inappropriate for a nun: AMOR VINCIT OMNIA (Love Conquers All). Such romantic formulae were not uncommon, for jewellery was seen as talismanic, and sometimes was made to commemorate betrothal or mourning. Usually a pious inscription is found, frequently a version of IHESUS NAZARENUS REX IUADAEORUM ('Jesus Christ, King of the Jews').

Jewellery was seen as a portable form of wealth, and there are fine hoards from Fishpool, Nottinghamshire, and Thame, Oxfordshire. The latter find included a reliquary ring and coins which provided a date for the deposition. The Fishpool hoard included a heart-shaped brooch of gold with blue and white enamel, which may have been a badge worn by a supporter of the Lancastrians in the Wars of the Roses.

The finest of all medieval brooches, The Dunstable Swan Jewel, was probably a Lancastrian badge of around 1460.

Bishops' rings have often survived, and include a series from Durham Cathedral and a fine example from Archbishop Walter de

Grey's tomb in York Minster. Bishops' rings had to be of pure gold and were blessed by the Pope. As they were worn over the glove they were of exceptional size.

Buckles and strap ends of all kinds are frequent finds on medieval sites, as are studs for decorating belts and the metal frames for purses that were hung from them.

Laws controlled who wore what by the mid fourteenth century. In 1363 legislation dictated that handcraftsmen and yeomen were not allowed to wear belts, brooches, garters, chains or seals of gold or silver. Knights were not permitted to wear rings or brooches of gold, or set with precious stones, and only esquires with land or rent of 200 marks a year or merchants and their families with goods or chattels worth £500 were allowed to wear clothes garnished with silver. In fact the legislation does not seem to have been enforced, but coincides with a greater interest in fashion, and an increase in the availability of gold. Jewellery was frequently imported from Paris at this time, and was used as security against loans.

Medieval buckles & belt fittings, mostly from the Thames foreshore (Lloyd Laing)

187

Gardens

Although there is evidence for gardening in Roman Britain, there is comparatively little for it during the Anglo-Saxon centuries. The Normans however were responsible for developments in horticulture, which was one of the activities associated with monasteries, particularly those of the Cistercian Order. The Cistercians were in particular concerned with the cultivation of fruit trees. A fire at Crowland Abbey in 1091 led to the destruction of ashes, oaks and willows, almost certainly deliberately planted. At Romsey Abbey flowers were being grown before 1092, while the refrectorer at Barnwell Priory, Cambridgeshire, was required in the twelfth century to furnish flowers, mint and fennel. Medieval watering cans are known, made of pottery with a narrow neck and perforated bottom. Once filled, the finger was kept over the mouth of the pot until the time was ripe for watering, when the finger was lifted and the air pressure caused the water to flow out of the holes at the bottom.

The Middle Ages also saw the proliferation of vineyards in England.

Henry of Huntingdon (d.1155) wrote eight books about plants, perfumes and gems. Pleasure gardens start to figure in accounts from the time of Henry I onwards, and included gardens laid out in London, for example at Clerkenwell, where walks were provided to offer shade.

An encyclopedia of gardening, compiled by Alexander Neckham (b.1157), listed some 140 species of plant. It includes some exotic herbage, such as date palm, mandrake, lemon, myrtle, orange and pomegranate. All these, though originally from other areas, seem to have been grown in Britain. Neckham also discussed cedar, chickpea, cork oak, cypress, ebony, nutmeg, olive and plane, though probably none of these was grown.

Among the flowers favoured in medieval gardens were roses: white, red and damask. The latter was the pink rose of Damascus. Medieval cultivated roses were delicately scented, and were of the nature of ramblers. The red rose petals were used to make rose water, rose oil and rose preserves. The lily, associated with the Virgin Mary, was also much favoured. The gillyflower, from which modern carnations are derived, was used both in cooking and as decoration, and was introduced by the Normans. Peonies were used medicinally, as well as being admired for their visual appeal.

The idea of a well-mown lawn was anathema to the medieval gardener. Grass was mown by scythe, and was liberally scattered with violets, daisies, primroses and periwinkles.

By the time of Edward I in the thirteenth century nurserymen in London were supplying seeds, onion sets, plants and grafted fruit trees. Others travelled round with packhorses laden with gardeners' needs.

Apples were clearly well liked since many varieties were grown — Pearmains, Bitter-sweets and Costards, for example. Popular pear varieties were Wardens, Caleols, Sorrells, and Gold Knopes. Cherries, plums and quinces were popular, and peaches were sometimes grown, though they were not easy to cultivate in Britain.

Pets were kept especially by the upper echelons of society, in order to prove conspicuously that they could afford to care for animals which did not earn their keep. Dogs were the most favoured, but there were unusual pets – a woman in the Luttrell Psalter (see p. 206) is shown with a squirrel wearing a collar to which a bell is fastened. The funeral effigy of Alice Cassy at Deerhurst, Glos, has at her feet her pet dog who is named Terri, while Sir Brian de Stapilton at Ingham, Norfolk has his pet called Jakke at his feet. A jolly dog, with a collar festooned with bells, appears grinning at the feet of Lady Margaret Roos in a stained glass window in York Minster.

Caged birds were also popular, the favourites being jays and magpies, the latter of which were taught to speak. Parrots (called popinjays) were imported at great cost from the Middle East. Nightingales and larks were much cheaper. St Hugh of Avalon, who came to England in 1180 to found a Carthusian house, had a pet swan which attacked all but its master.

Cats were practical pets, since they dealt with mice and rats, and also seem to have been kept on occasions for their fur. At Exeter Cathedral between 1305 and 1467 a cat was paid a penny a week to catch unwelcome intruders, and was furnished with a cat-hole in the door of the north transept wall.

Effigy of a knight and his lady,
c.1400 (Joan Nunn)

9 · Intellectual and Artistic Endeavour

OPPOSITE: *Chaucer reading from* Troilus & Criseyde, *early 15th century, MS 61, f. 1v (Corpus Christi College Library, Cambridge)*

LITERATURE, music, philosophy, theology, art and education in general had been developing rapidly under the late Saxons, reaching considerable heights just before the Conquest. The devastation caused by the Normans, the determination of their successors to expand their territory to include areas never under Saxon domination, and their inability to stabilize the throne meant that cultural life was constantly shaken up. The general effect however was to slow rather than to stifle completely: outside stimuli from foreign wars and contacts brought new ideas to compensate for all the money lost in warfare that might have been channelled into culture.

Schools and Universities

In the Middle Ages education was the province of the Church, and so the subjects taught were those which were appropriate to ecclesiastical ends. The teachers were clerics, and elementary education consisted of reading, singing, and religious instruction. Nunneries were often at the forefront of this, but there were also schools attached to cathedrals and to churches. Grammar Schools were founded in order to teach Latin grammar and prose composition, and to prepare pupils for university where theological studies could begin in earnest.

What was taught in nunnery schools is difficult to determine, though it would seem that boys and girls were taught together. That they did not always have their minds on higher things is suggested by a poem by Froissart (1338–1410), in which he says he went to school to learn Latin at the age of twelve but neglected his studies to give presents of pins, apples, pears, and glass rings to little girls sitting on his bench. This led to letting his mind wander to what it would be like to be grown-up and making love to them.

Not everyone thought that an ecclesiastical education was paramount for getting on in life. Private teachers in late medieval Oxford ran what may be termed 'law schools', where in addition to teaching Latin and French, instruction was given in conveyancing, accounting, legal pleading and the drawing up of wills. In London in the fourteenth century there was a lawyers' university centred on the Inns of Court. In 1385 the first English school to be founded by a layman was established.

Girls did not go to grammar schools, as Latin grammar was not deemed essential to their upbringing, but sometimes went to song schools and also were taught at home both the practical skills of estate management (including basic law and accounts) and the principles of running a household, including polished manners and proper deportment. To aid them in such studies, manuals were written, such as the Book of the *Knight of La Tour-Landry*, a French work of the later fourteenth century. The object of all this instruction was to increase the marriageability of the girl in question.

Such young ladies were in fact sometimes taught Latin, and mothers were known to make their own textbooks to instruct their children. Some ladies went on to acquire notable libraries: one such was Joan Beaufort, duchess of Westmorland, who lent her nephew Henry V two books around 1410, which he forgot to return. Some of the owners of libraries had a special interest in books by women, such as the fifteenth-century Alice Chaucer, duchess of Suffolk, and Cecily Neville, duchess of York.

There was, of course, much hostility towards the education of women. Clerics believed that women who had been taught to read and write would spend their time composing love letters and reading heretical literature. In the 1350s, a French noble Bertrand du Guesclin said 'in women there is no more sense than there is in a sheep', a sentiment that would have found supporters in England, where one visitor noted that 'the working of a woman's wit is considered of small account'.

Such prejudices however were usually irrelevant since the main obstacle to education was money. Even many clerics were pathetically uneducated, and since books were immensely costly, most learning had to be by oral communication and by rote learning. The increasing use of paper (which had been introduced from the East in the twelfth century) meant that books became cheaper since much of the cost lay in the price of vellum.

Universities originated on the Continent, and the model for medieval universities was Paris. The first university in England was Oxford, where before 1150 there were a number of learned men living and teaching. By the beginning of the thirteenth century there were about 1500 students there. Cambridge was established not long after Oxford. Both universities became collegiate institutions in the thirteenth century, and were further increased by an exodus of scholars from Paris. Universities were not popular with the laity, who thought that there was no call for so much academic theology and who believed the students to be wild and disreputable. In Cambridge in 1381 university manuscripts were burned by the townspeople – a townswoman, Margery Starre, threw the ashes in the air shouting, 'Away with the learning of clerks!'

The accusation regarding students may not have been totally unfounded. An Oxford statute of 1432 ruled against those who,

sleep all day and by night haunt the taverns and brothels for occasions of robbery and manslaughter – therefore it is decreed by the said university that all and every scholar shall dwell in that Hall or College wherein his common contributions are registered.

EXPLICIVNT CAP̄L̄A IN IEREMIĀ PROPHL̄:
INCIPIT LIBER IEREMIE PROPHETE :·

FILII HELCHIE DE SACERDO
tibus qui fuerunt in anathoth interra beniamin.
quod factum est uerbum dn̄i ad eum indiebus
iosie filii amon regis iuda · intertio decimo an
no regni eius · & factum est indiebus ioachim

In the same year fines were established to be imposed on students

for drawing of weapons of violence or for thrusting with shoulder or striking with fist, 4s; for striking with stone or staff, 6s 8d; for striking with knife, dagger, baselard or sword, with axe or any such weapon of war, 10s; for bearing of a bow and shooting therewith with intent to harm, 20s.

The university also had to ban the playing of tennis and other ball games in the streets and within the college precincts.

Others were more dedicated. A life of Sir Richard of Chichester said he preferred his studies to a good marriage:

Such was his love of learning, that he cared little for food or raiment. For, as he was wont to relate, he and two companions who lodged in the same chamber had only their tunics, and one gown between them, and each of them a miserable pallet. When one, therefore, went out with the gown to hear a lecture, the others sat in their room, and so they went forth alternately; and bread with a little wine and pottage sufficed for their food. (Quoted in Coulton, *Social Life in Britain from the Conquest to the Reformation*, 1918, 61).

Literature

The Norman Conquest established a new language in England; French. Since the leaders of the Church and most of the nobility were Norman incomers, French came to replace English as the language of the great and the good, and also became the language of trade. It was additionally the language most often chosen for creative writing. That is not to say that Anglo-Saxon disappeared, for it remained the tongue of the majority of the population, but in the Norman and Angevin period English ceased to be the language used for the written word, and gradually more and more words of French derivation were added to the native vocabulary as Middle English developed from Old English after 1066. Although there were different dialects of English spoken in the Middle Ages, the Standard seems to have been that spoken in the west Midlands, around Hereford. Chaucer spoke a west Midland dialect, even though he was born and died in London.

Scholars and clerics opted for Latin — it was the international language of the Church, and was also the language of officialdom. It was used in the courts, in diplomatic correspondence, in charters and writs, though French seems to have been the vernacular counterpart in such circles.

Anglo-French (or Anglo-Norman) was used extensively in writing from the time of Henry I to the time of Henry IV, when the hostility to France engendered by the Hundred Years War led to the increased use of English, French being mostly used from this time on in Parliament and courts. In 1385 one writer accounted for the decline of French in terms of the effects of the Black Death, which he saw as killing off French teachers. In 1362 English became the language of law courts, and in 1363 the Chancellor opened Parliament in English. The first will in English dates from 1387. By the late fifteenth century even ambassadors to France spoke English rather than French.

In the twelfth century there were a number of religious works written in Anglo-French, and during the thirteenth and fourteenth centuries a series of manuals were produced in the language on such diverse subjects as agriculture, medicine, law, grammar, courtly manners, hawking and chess. For those who had trouble with the orthography, there were even from the late thirteenth century books written to improve spelling.

After the Conquest academic interest in Old English led to the copying of a number of Anglo-Saxon manuscripts, including a text of one of Alfred the Great's works that is not known from an earlier version. Some writs were still set down in English. The most notable work in English at this time however was the continuing *Anglo-Saxon Chronicle*. This had originally been compiled in the time of Alfred as a year-by-year account of events. Copies of the text were sent to several major monasteries, which then updated the account with the passage of time and events. Of particular note is the version compiled at Peterborough, which was regularly updated until 1254, and contains a dramatic account of the Anarchy of Stephen (see p. 11). English was also used for some devotional writing.

In the period following the conquest too, a tradition of historical writing in Latin flourished in England, of which the work of William of Malmesbury is notable. By the twelfth century historical fact was merged with literary fiction by Geoffrey of Monmouth, whose *History of the Kings of Britain* was a factor in the development of Arthurian legend.

Much of the verse current in England was Anglo-Norman. The English do not seem to have favoured the chivalric form known as the *Chanson de Geste* for original compositions, though the earliest surviving version of the great French cycle about Charlemagne, the *Chanson de Roland*, is in Anglo-French. There are however many romances of the twelfth century in the language, which continued to be written into the thirteenth century.

Bone writing tablet, with romantic scene, late 14th century (Southampton Museum)

It was in Layamon's *Brut* that England had its first native Arthurian tale – inspired by Geoffrey of Monmouth via a French translation, it turned to Anglo-Saxon heroic ideals and chose to ignore the chivalric overlay of contemporary French literature about the hero.

A popular cycle of stories in medieval England concerned Reynard the Fox. This satirical fable was a popular theme for artists seeking subject matter (for example in the carving of misericords), and appeared first as the story of 'The Fox and the Wolf'. Other popular stories included one about Havelok the Dane, a Danish prince who disguised himself as a Grimsby fisherman's son and eventually regained his inheritance.

Lyrics were an innovation of the medieval period, and included 'Mirie it is while sumer ilast' (written c.1225) and the well known 'Sumer is icumen in'.

*15C quarries from Wells Cathedral —
used as a surround for more strongly
coloured glass (Dean and Chapter of
Wells)*

English literature burgeoned from the mid fourteenth century, when long, alliterative poems became fashionable. Much of this has survived, and it continued to be produced in Scotland until the sixteenth century. In the late fourteenth century (*c.*1370) the *Vision of Piers Ploughman* was composed. This is usually attributed to William Langland, a long and complex allegory which despite some of its linguistic crudities is deservedly one of the most esteemed of English poems.

Arthurian romance inspired another medieval masterpiece, *Sir Gawain and the Green Knight*. This is a tale rich in language and subtle in its moral undertones and psychological understanding. It contains some Northern English dialect.

Scottish literature too seems to have developed in the fourteenth century, well exemplified at this time in Barbour's *Bruce* (finished 1376), a patriotic epic poem influenced by northern English trends.

Geoffrey Chaucer (*c.*1342–1400), the most famous of medieval English writers, was a court poet. Chaucer came from a prosperous middle-class background – his father was a vintner. As a court official on diplomatic missions, he travelled widely in Flanders, France and Italy, and was a close friend of Henry IV. Chaucer borrowed heavily from French and developed from it the ten-syllable line. He also pioneered the 'rime royal' (stanzas of seven lines) in his *Parliament of Fowles*. His greatest works were *Troilus and Criseyde* and the *Canterbury Tales*. The latter, modelled on Boccaccio's *Decameron*, is a collection of stories, mostly traditional, narrated by pilgrims on their way from London to Canterbury.

An older contemporary court-poet was John Gower; later imitators of Chaucer included John Lydgate.

The fifteenth century saw the development of a variety of other literary forms, such as Christmas carols, and the proliferation of mystery plays.

In the late fifteenth century the most notable writer was Sir Thomas Mallory, whose *Morte d'Arthur* was finished in 1470 and printed by William Caxton in 1485.

In Scotland, Chaucer inspired the 'Scottish Chaucerians': Robert Henryson, William Dunbar, Gavin Douglas and Sir David Lyndsay, who carried medieval traditions on into the sixteenth century.

Music

There was both secular and ecclesiastical music. Medical theory argued that music could aid healing by promoting tranquility, and music was believed to promote the consummation of marriage.

Medieval music was monophonic, but by the early thirteenth century polyphony was subject to experimentation. Key to an understanding of medieval music is plainsong, and the notation for recording this was developed around AD 800. 'Pricksongs' were songs written down with a notation, and became common by the fifteenth century. For early fifteenth-century music there is a collection of pieces by at least 25 composers set down in the early fifteenth century – The Old Hall Manuscript.

Instruments included the harp, with up to fifteen strings of sheep gut. The psaltery was similarly open-stringed. This had metal strings, plucked with a quill plectrum. The gittern was the northern equivalent of the guitar, and like the citole had four strings. Also stringed was the rebec, the fiddle and the rotta, a kind of late medieval lyre. The harpsichord came in at the end of the Middle Ages, as did the symphony (hurdy-gurdy). Wind instruments included the bagpipe, shawm, bombard and the organ.

Art

Patronage of the arts requires wealth and focus, and in the Middle Ages the wealth, as has been seen, was concentrated in the hands of a few: Church, nobility and rich merchants.

However, the focus of art was notably narrow, being mostly devoted to religious matters and created by artists and craftspeople who had been trained by the Church. The patrons were rich people whose objective was to gain not only contemporaneous admiration, but more particularly everlasting favour in the eyes of God. As a result, the majority of extant artworks remain in the ecclesiastical buildings for which they were created. It was not until the Renaissance that the concept of elevating non-spiritual and non-religious subjects through art became prevalent.

Artistic endeavour survives in textiles, embroideries, sculpture, metalwork, wall paintings, painted glasswork, manuscripts and wood. A number of different artistic styles developed throughout the Middle Ages.

Styles of art   The arrival of the Normans marked the beginning of a period of transition in English art. Before the Conquest there had flourished in southern England one of the finest traditions of art in western Europe. This had been focused particularly on Winchester (though there were several other centres in the south), and was particularly notable for drawing and the production of tinted outline work. One of the pioneers in the tenth century had been St Dunstan, one of whose drawings still survives, and a range of manuscripts had been produced ranging from the sumptuous Benedictional of St Aethelwold to more modest but equally vigorous works. The Winchester style as it has been termed flourished not only in manuscripts, but in ivory carvings and rather less notably in stone sculpture.

In the north of England, where the Scandinavian impact was particularly strong, another, Anglo-Scandinavian art can be found, primarily in sculptured crosses which combine elements of Viking and Anglo-Saxon art.

The Norman Conquest did not put an end to the traditions of Anglo-Saxon art, though the Norman arrival probably speeded up the assimilation of Continental Romanesque traditions which were already beginning to make their mark. At the same time Viking art styles subtly pervaded southern English art. The Urnes style of Scandinavian art, characterized by fleshy tendrils, can be seen for example on the door-

way of the church at Kilpeck, Hereford, built around 1140, or on the bronze crosier of Ranulf Flambard in Durham Cathedral.

An element of the Winchester style that remained popular with the Normans was acanthus foliage – the acanthus being a Mediterranean plant, which was popular on both sides of the Channel from the tenth century onwards as a decorative detail.

Manuscripts

The penmanship of Winchester drawing had been growing more ponderous just before the Conquest, a trend which continued after it, although English Romanesque art was always lighter than its Continental counterparts.

The Normans turned away from full-page biblical illustrations to what has been termed the 'historiated initial' – elaborate initials, often infilled with complex scenes. The historiated initial was not new – the Winchester artists used it from time to time – but the Normans made it theirs. In the same way the Normans favoured less splendid books (though they still continued to produce some of these from the early twelfth century onwards), and a new hybrid artistic style grew up on either side of the English Channel which art historians have termed the 'Channel style'. This was mainly a phenomenon of northern France, the Low Countries, and the south coast of England.

By the early twelfth century a greater attention to naturalism was spreading from Continental Romanesque art. A particular device was the 'damp fold', which spread from the Byzantine world first to Italy then the rest of Europe. This, as the name suggests, employed a particularly subtle type of drapery, and first appears in England in the Bury Bible, the work of Master Hugo of Bury St Edmunds.

The twelfth century was the golden age of the great Bibles. Of these, the finest were the Winchester and Bury Bibles, with the Carilef Bible a runner-up.

Some other fine twelfth-century manuscripts were produced apart from Bibles. Of these can be singled out the Albani Psalter.

In the thirteenth century, manuscript art continued the tradition of fine drawing that had originated in the Anglo-Saxon period. The greatest exponent at this time was Matthew Paris, who worked in St Albans Abbey and who drew not just ecclesiastical subjects but sketches of things that he had observed, such as the elephant brought for Henry III's menagerie.

In this period the figures became tall and willowy, with loose-fitting garments which provided the kind of flowing draperies thirteenth-century artists loved. Good examples in the style are the Evesham Psalter and the Guthlac Roll.

Between 1270 and 1370 foliage became more natural, and figures became more elegant. Backgrounds were more sumptuous, with the use of gold and repeated patterns. With the reign of Henry III English manuscript art passed into the High Gothic, well represented in the Oscott Psalter and the de Lisle Psalter. Some of these manuscripts have a wealth of detail which sheds light on real life in medieval Britain.

ABOVE: *Malmesbury, tympanum in porch, depicting apostles, c.1155–65 (Philip Dixon)*

RIGHT: *Effigy of Alice de la Pole, d.1475, Ewelme, Oxfordshire (Philip Dixon)*

OPPOSITE: *Medieval wall paintings, Blyth, Nottinghamshire (Philip Dixon)*

Alabaster carving of the Holy Trinity, c.1400 (Victoria & Albert Museum)

Among these, the Luttrell Psalter is of exceptional interest. Commissioned by Sir Geoffrey Luttrell of Lincolnshire (b.1276), it contains countless scenes from domestic and public life.

The fourteenth and fifteenth centuries saw the production of outstanding manuscripts, rich in colour and imagery. Gold backgrounds were a feature of many of these, and in East Anglia in particular in the fourteenth century magnificent psalters were produced with rich decorative details including grotesque creatures and plant motifs.

Sculpture

Most Norman sculpture in England is fragmentary, but is seen at its best adorning buildings. The Anglo-Saxons had employed architectural sculpture, but never as successfully as the Normans. Some stone was imported from Caen, and later from Tournai, but mostly the materials used were native. The Normans excelled at decorating column capitals, and nowhere can this be seen to better effect than in the crypt of Canterbury Cathedral, where the capitals display animals playing musical instruments. Fine capitals also come from Reading Abbey, Berkshire.

The Normans developed the Romanesque tympanum – a sculptured panel inset over a doorway. Continental cathedrals were furnished with powerful tympana depicting the Last Judgement, for example at Moissac and Autun, but in England tympana show great diversity, including some with Anglo-Scandinavian influence, such as those at Southwell and Hoveringham, Notts. Christ in Majesty is the focus of the magnificent tympana at Malmesbury, Wiltshire (c.1160), Ely (c.1140) and Rochester (c.1180). Of the other sculptures of the period, particular mention may be made of the Chichester Reliefs, which are sculptural renderings of the Channel style and display Christ carrying his cross and the raising of Lazarus.

During the thirteenth century, sculpture was not as distinguished on the whole as that found in France, but there are some fine figures on the west front of Wells Cathedral, and in the transepts of Westminster Abbey. A series of figures from St Mary's Abbey, York, of the first decade of the thirteenth century, are similarly noteworthy for their Gothic naturalism and fine draperies. The Angel Choir of Lincoln Cathedral (c.1270–80) marks the solid style of the first manifestations of High Gothic.

Tomb sculpture was a notable achievement of the age (see p. 210). Some Purbeck marble was employed in tomb reliefs, and in the Midlands, particularly at Nottingham, alabaster was carved. Some bronze funereal effigies are found, such as those of Henry III and his daughter-in-law, in Westminster Abbey. Among the other major funereal effigies can be singled out one of William Longespee, in Salisbury cathedral, dated to c.1230–40, and among architectural details may be mentioned a stone head from the Clarendon Palace, Wiltshire, of c.1240.

Architectural details   Squints were openings made through walls to allow a view of an altar, usually the High Altar. Some were intended

to allow the bell-ringer to see the High Altar so that he knew when to ring the sanctus bell. Debate has surrounded the function of so-called 'leper windows', which were not, as popularly believed, to allow lepers to see a service, or for confession, as is also sometimes suggested. It is more likely that they were to allow a bell to be rung at Sanctus and at the Consecration of the Elements. They are usually found at the west end of the chancel. The lower part was often covered by a shutter, which still survives at Melton Constable, Norfolk.

Frequently in the chancel wall, usually on the south side near the High Altar, can be found one or more piscinas — drains in a niche, usually surmounted by a decorative arch. These enabled the liturgical vessels to be washed, and the officiating priest to rinse his hands. A double piscina was a feature generally of the time of Edward I, when separate drains were deemed essential for each function, and a good example can be seen at Cherry Hinton, Cambridgeshire.

Lincoln Cathedral, early Gothic capitals in the east transept (Edwin Smith)

207

Altars   In the later Middle Ages there was a proliferation of altars, where masses could be said for the souls of those who had endowed the church, located in chantry chapels, such as that in Newark, Notts. By this period too there was a clutter of relics and statues of saints.

Fonts   Norman fonts survive in considerable numbers. They were large, as total immersion was the custom at baptism in this period. They are frequently sculptured, with monsters and Old and New Testament scenes. There are some notable examples in the East Riding of Yorkshire (e.g. Cowlam), in north-west Norfolk (e.g. South Wootton), in Herefordshire (e.g. Castle Frome) and in Cornwall (e.g. Bodmin). They are usually carved from local stone, but about thirty are of lead ·and seven made of imported Tournai marble (a good example is in Winchester Cathedral).

OPPOSITE: *15c transept window of Great Malvern Priory (Patrick Reyntiens)*

Font, c.1140–50, Castle Frome, Somerset (Philip Dixon)

The normal shape for a Norman font was circular or square. In the Transitional period between Norman and Early English there are square bowls supported on a central shaft with four corner-supporting shafts.

In the fourteenth century the preferred shape was octagonal, with niches and sometimes tracery (for example at Brailes, Warwickshire). In the fifteenth century fonts were frequently set on steps, the best being found in East Anglia, and include a group with the Seven Sacraments, with another scene on the eighth side, for instance at Gresham, Norfolk. Some, for example Westhall, Suffolk retain traces of paint.

Since holy water was sometimes pilfered from the fonts, covers were devised to protect it. Most fonts retain only the staples, but a few have wooden covers, for example at Monksilver, Somerset.

In East Anglia a pinnacled drum was favoured. Some can be very ornate: that at Ufford, Suffolk, is crowned with a pelican, and was originally painted and gilded. Some font covers were suspended from a special beam, or were raised and lowered by a crane (for example the one at Sall, Norfolk).

*Angel in the south transept of
Westminster Abbey, London, c.1254–8
(National Monuments Record)*

Many fine covers worked on a telescopic principle, with a counter-
poise inside the upper part of the cover over which the lower part tele-
scopes.

Memorials   Various types of memorial are found in churches and
churchyards. Among the most distinctive are effigies and brasses. The
former were carved from alabaster (quarried in the Midlands), stone,
(including Purbeck marble), wood and sometimes bronze. Bronze
monuments are the rarest: apart from royal monuments in Westminster
Abbey, the only others are the tomb of the Black Prince in Canterbury
Cathedral and that of Richard Beauchamp in St Mary's, Warwick. That
of the Black Prince has his helm, shield and other honours suspended
above it.

Many of these monuments had a canopy above them, such as that
of Edmund Crouchback in Westminster Abbey, or the Percy monument in Beverly Minster, Yorkshire. Frequently the tomb has little
figures round the sides called weepers, who may be family members or

Lincoln Cathedral, early Gothic carving at the doorway to the south choir aisle (Edwin Smith)

angels. At Strelley, Nottinghamshire, Sir Samson de Strelley and his wife lie hand in hand on a tomb of about 1400.

From the thirteenth century grave-slabs incised with a cross became common. In the fifteenth century and later incised portraits of the deceased were carved on the grave slab on occasion. Small monuments sometimes mark the place where a heart is buried, for example at Youlgreave, Derbys.

Perhaps the most famous of all medieval funerary monuments however are the monumental brasses. Made of latten metal (copper and tin with a high lead content), the material was imported from Flanders and Germany. In England the sheets of latten were cut out and embedded in stone or Purbeck marble, in contrast to the Continental custom of engraving a complete sheet. The earliest surviving is that of Sir John Daubernoon at Stoke D'Abernon, Surrey, datable to 1277. The earliest brass of a woman is of Margaret de Camoys at Trotton, Sussex (*c.*1310).

The earliest brasses were usually crosses or half-figures with inscriptions in Lombardic (i.e. rounded) lettering, inadequately attached

Enamelled silver diptych, c.1335–45, with scenes from the life of Christ (Victoria & Albert Museum)

to their slabs with pitch. Later medieval brasses were thinner, but fastened with rivets into lead-filled holes in the stone. The earlier brasses are nearly always life-size and deeply and carefully cut. Palimpsest brasses are those that have been re-used, usually by adding a new inscription or by altering the figure slightly. More often a 'second-hand' brass was turned over and engraved with a new design on the back.

Brasses provide a gallery of fashion, of changing styles of arms and armour in the later Middle Ages. Sometimes however archaic fashions appear, due to the use of old pattern books, so the fashions on brasses are not an invariable guide to date.

Centres for the production of brasses are known to have existed in York, Lincoln, Shrewsbury and London as well as probably elsewhere.

Church Plate and Crosses

Later in the thirteenth century statutes required that churches should possess amongst other things, chalices, a ciborium (for holding the sacramental bread), a pyx (for the reserved sacrament), a chrismatory (for holy oils), an incense boat, three cruets and a holy water vessel.

The Palm Sunday procession celebrated in Jerusalem was imitated in medieval churches, and resulted in the erection of churchyard crosses. Sometimes these have a niche to hold the ciborium during the last station before the procession entered the church. The multiplication of doors in churches was similarly connected with processions.

Church walls were plastered and usually painted. Comparatively few wall paintings have survived, due to the Victorian delight in stripping walls down to the stonework, which the medieval builders never intended to be seen. In the same way the exteriors of buildings were plastered and in some cases painted to resemble stonework – in 1868 evidence came to light in excavation that York Minster once had exterior plastering of this kind. The wall paintings, which belong to all periods from the twelfth century, were not intended simply as decoration, but as a means of reinforcing devotion and instructing the congregation (of whom 95 per cent would have been illiterate) in biblical and other suitably uplifting stories. The quality of the art was of very little importance, though many wall paintings were in fact executed by skilled artists. Some seem to have been produced by schools, centred on major churches or monasteries, for example St Albans, where Matthew Paris flourished in the thirteenth century, Norwich, Canterbury, Peterborough, Winchester and Westminster, the focus for the 'Court' School. Some of the artists were monks, some were laymen. Walter of Colchester was mentioned by Matthew Paris as an incomparable painter, and Matthew Paris himself, who was a Benedictine monk at St Albans, was commissioned to work for the king. Laymen such as Master Walter and Master Peter also figure among the names of artists working for the king at Westminster, Clarendon Palace and elsewhere. Conventions dictated the interpretation of the scenes, and particular gestures were immediately recognizable. Thus a curved, apparently beckoning finger, meant the figure was speaking; up-raised hands represented argument; hands and arms outspread lower down signified wonder, adoration or listening, depending on the context. Crossed legs were a sign of wickedness, as the stance interrupted the flow of life. The soul was represented as a naked figure, sometimes wearing headgear appropriate to the deceased's status (such as a mitre). The costume depicted was that current at the time of the painting, which facilitated immediate recognition of rank. Episodes in stories were sometimes conflated.

Some of the wall paintings were simply decorative, but most were biblical or episodes from saints' lives – St Christopher and St George figure quite prominently, as do St Nicholas and St Anne. Sequences of pictures relating to the Virgin probably adorned the walls in most churches adjacent to the Lady Altar. Many of the later cycles of paintings were based on the *Legenda Aurea* (Golden Legend) of Jacobus de Voragine, Archbishop of Genoa, compiled in the thirteenth century. Other popular subjects included morality tales and depictions of the Last Judgement. Among warnings given are those against swearing and against idle gossip. A lost window at Heydon, Norfolk, depicted figures swearing 'By God's bones that was good ale', and 'By the feet of Christ I will beat you at dice', among other blasphemies. Zodiac signs and labours of the months also figure sometimes.

Incised designs also appear in some churches. There are three categories: masons' marks, symbols and graffiti. Masons' marks are designs, usually of a few incised lines, used to record masons' work and probably intended as a record of particular mason's output. They were a method of monitoring building operations. They are found in churches all over Britain; detailed study of those in Lincoln Cathedral, for example, has shed much light on the building programme in the Angel Choir there. Symbols are comparatively rare, and are complex designs that appear with little variation in widely dispersed buildings. They may have been the badges of a religious or knightly order. They include such designs as complex knots of interlace, for example the so-called swastika-pelta that appears at St John's Church, Duxford, Cambridgeshire, and many other buildings. It is a Christian symbol of considerable antiquity widely distributed in Europe, and occurs for example in wall paintings at Stoke Orchard church, Gloucestershire.

Graffiti

Graffiti are particularly common in churches, less so in castles. They are found widely in England, but are less common in Scotland and rarer still in Wales. Typically, they were sketched on the smooth surfaces of columns or dressed stone expanses on the inside of buildings. Very often they seem to have been carried out before the surface was plastered or painted, and they can retain traces in the incisions of the plaster or paint that later covered them.

Most commonly they were executed with a fine stylus, though some seem to have been chiselled, and, as with Palaeolithic cave engravings, it is sometimes difficult to distinguish designs due to overlays. As far as they can be dated, from details of lettering, clothing or other clues, they span the period from the twelfth to the sixteenth century. From the fourteenth century onwards, a few bear actual dates.

Some of the graffiti were clearly the work of architects and masons since they comprise architectural sketches of details and elevations. In Rosslyn Chapel, Midlothian, a sketch of Gothic arches adorns the wall of the crypt, while at Ely Cathedral the inside walls of the 'Galilee Porch' are marked by masons' sketches which include one of the gable with pinnacled side turrets, which no longer exists.

The subject matter of graffiti is very varied. They include caricatures, animals, staves of music, armorial crests, figures of warriors and musicians, domestic vessels, ships and abstract designs.

From the point of view of the modern observer, however, perhaps the most endearing graffiti are caricatures and sketches which reveal something of the medieval sense of humour. Some of them resemble stills from modern animated cartoons — take for instance the drawing at Harlton, Cambridgeshire, assumed to be a depiction of Henry V at the time of his Coronation in 1413. It makes him look not unlike the cartoon character Bart Simpson, though whether the humour is deliberate or simply due to incompetence is difficult to say. The Man in the Moon, done in a deliberately humorous style, appears in the same church.

At Stetchworth, also in Cambridgeshire, there is a pair of graffiti, one showing a lady of fashion with an elaborate head-dress of fourteenth-century style. Adjacent is a drawing of an owl with similarly elaborate head-dress. In the Middle Ages owls were regarded as extremely stupid, and the second drawing may be a comment on the first. In the same church is a drawing of a man in thirteenth-century French dress, and two drawings of animals, one of a cat's face in a square, the other of a bird. At Gamlingay, Cambridgeshire, caricatures of two heads wearing fourteenth-century headgear appear to be drawn from life, while at Stoke-by-Clare in Suffolk a caricatured man plays a shawm – a type of medieval oboe.

Some motifs recur in many buildings. These have been interpreted as the badges of medieval religious or knightly orders. A complex inter-laced design known as the 'swastika pelta' occurs widely in eastern England, and may be connected with the Knights Templar (see p. 100). Fleurs de lys, also common symbols, were probably symbols of the Virgin Mary.

Graffito at Harlton, Cambs, presumed to be of Henry V

History comes alive at Ashwell, Hertfordshire, where graffiti on the wall of the church idiosyncratically record that 'The beginning of the plague was in 1350 minus one'.

Lower down in a different hand, we learn,

49/ pestilence that is five/1350 wretched, fierce, violent/1350/the dregs of the populace live to tell the tale. At the end of the second [pestilence] a mighty wind/this year Maurus thunders in the heavens 1361.

The latter is a contemporary allusion to the Black Death.

The same church has a detailed drawing of a church, variously intepreted as old St Paul's (replaced by Wren) or the transept of Westminster Abbey.

Graffiti are also encountered on cave walls and pieces of stone. At King's Cave in Arran graffiti of many different periods include several of medieval date including one of a man on horseback. From the seventh century onwards the Celtic areas have yielded sketches on pieces of stone and bone which are commonly termed motif pieces. Some were preliminary sketches for art work, some were apprentices' exercises, others were simply 'doodles'.

Of the later medieval examples a particularly curious series comes from Tintagel in Cornwall. These include a sketch of an exotic turtle, occasionally found in Cornish waters, and another of a boat. Two frag-ments of slate from the site of the manor house at Mudgley, near Wells, Somerset, have a passage of music on them.

Stained Glass

Stained (or, more correctly, painted) glass windows served a similar function to wall paintings, and have a comparable spread of dates from the twelfth century onwards. In windows however there is little scope for narrative cycles, and the subject matter has to be more direct and simpler. Stained glass is encountered in the Anglo-Saxon monas-teries of Monkwearmouth and Jarrow, and survives from all periods from the twelfth century onwards.

Medieval glass became widespread following Abbot Suger of

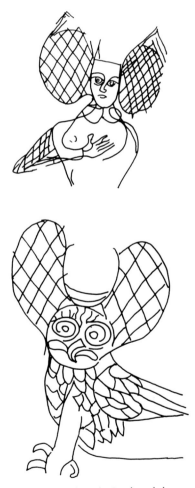

Graffiti at Stetchworth, Cambs: a lady compared to an owl

St Denis' (France) pronouncements on light, and the effect was of jewelled brilliance. There is good twelfth century glass at Canterbury Cathedral and at Dorchester Abbey. For thirteenth-century glass Canterbury is also important. At this time grisaille glass was introduced — white glass with foliage patterns arranged so that the lead strips made part of the design. In the fourteenth century picture panels on a grisaille ground were widespread, for example at Merton College, Oxford. Up to this time, too, each colour had to be leaded separately, but subsequently a method was devised of abrading the colour to show the clear glass underneath. Additionally, a yellow stain was discovered that could be painted on to white or coloured glass.

At this period heraldry started to be employed in windows (it appears very occasionally in wall paintings), and figures are given an S-curve to their bodies. Particularly good work of this period can be seen at York Minster. Fifteenth-century glass used lighter colours, and the long panels of Perpendicular windows allowed for better figural work. Subjects found in glass include the Seven Sacraments, Seven Works of Mercy, Nine Orders of Angels, and the Tree of Jesse.

Glazed floor tiles

Glazed floor tiles are first encountered in the Anglo-Saxon period. In the medieval period some were shaped into lozenges, discs and arches to make tile mosaics. Others were line-impressed, with patterns raised on the moulds to make incised linear designs on the tiles — subjects included lion heads and in one case (from Norton Priory, Cheshire) the depiction of grape treading. Some were fired red and inlaid with patterns in white clay. When glazed and fired they give a brown and yellow appearance.

Each tile could hold part of an overall design requiring several tiles. A development (long before the printing press) consisted of a design which was printed in different coloured clay on the tile surface.

Some tiles were richly pictorial, such as those from the Chertsey Abbey, which depict figures including Saladin and others from the story of Richard I and episodes from the romance of Tristram and Isolde.

Carved wood

In early medieval churches there was no seating for the congregation, though sometimes a bench was provided along the wall for the elderly and infirm (hence the expression, 'the weakest go to the wall'). From the thirteenth century onwards however wooden benches were increasingly provided, the ends of which were sometimes richly carved.

The most common design was the 'poppy head' bench end (the 'poppy' probably comes from *puppis*, the figure head of a ship), beneath which reliefs of figures or animals were sometimes displayed. Most of these date from the fifteenth century. The best examples are to be found in East Anglia and the west of England.

Detail from a misericord in Ely Cathedral choir (Edwin Smith)

Three bench ends at Brent Knoll, Somerset, tell the fable of Reynard the Fox, disguised as a mitred abbot.

Misericords   Misericords were carved wooden tip-up stall seats with projections on the underside to provide some repose when standing.

The main projection has two subsidiary carvings called supporters. Very large numbers survive in the larger churches, for example at Boston, Lincolnshire, Chester Cathedral, Ludlow in Shropshire, Lincoln Cathedral and Worcester Cathedral.

The symbolism of the carvings is very complex, though there is usually a simple superficial explanation. Owls, as has been noted, were not regarded as wise but foolish, and represented the Jews. The pelican was believed to peck its breast to give blood to its young, as Christ gave his blood for humans. A king between two griffins at Wells cathedral represented Alexander the Great.

Humorous and wise sayings also figure. The story of Reynard the Fox, the Romance of Alexander, satires on monks and doctors, everyday occupations, activities of the months and many other subjects are to be found. Many were inspired by the *Biblia Pauperum*, (Poor Man's Bible), a picture book version of the Bible that appeared around 1300, and the Bestiary, a book of animals.

217

Eve spinning, Adam digging. A miseri-cord in Worcester Cathedral choir, c.1379 (by permission of the Dean and Chapter of Worcester)

Rood screens (which were used to display crucifixes in front of Altars) were usually of wood, and richly carved then gilded and painted. They date from the thirteenth century onwards, and there are particularly fine examples in Devon.

Secular interior decoration and furniture

Generally speaking, secular interior decoration has not survived or was less sumptuous than ecclesiastical.

Carpets were introduced to England by Eleanor of Castille, as were baths. Matthew Paris noted of the Spaniards in the thirteenth century that,

The manners of the Spaniards were utterly at variance with English customs and habits; that while the walls of their lodgings in the Temple were hung with silks and tapestry, and the very floors covered with costly carpets, their retinue was vulgar and disorderly; they had few horses and many mules.

The Liberate Rolls of Henry III give some information about interior decoration. Thus the Sheriff of Wiltshire was given the order to make alterations to the King's palace at Clarendon, to

wainscote the King's lower chamber, and to paint the wainscote of a green colour, and to put a border to it, and to cause the heads of kings and queens to be painted on the borders; and to paint on the walls of the king's upper chamber the story of St Margaret Virgin, and the four Evangelists; and to paint the wainscote of the same chamber of a green colour, spotted with gold, and to paint on it heads of men and women; and all these paintings to be done with good and exquisite colours.

Around the same period the keeper of the King's works at Westminster was commanded to

raise the chimney of the queen's chamber, and to paint the chimney of the chamber aforesaid, and on it to be portrayed a figure of Winter, which as well by its sad countenance as by other miserable distortions of the body may be deservedly likened to Winter itself.

Windows were not generally glazed, but were protected by shutters, and furniture mainly consisted of chests, heavy chairs, forms and tables.

Textiles and embroideries

Textiles were of great importance in the Middle Ages, and could often be very costly. Particularly expensive were embroideries. The embroiderers who mostly worked in London, in the mid fourteenth century were paid 12d per day (designers), 3d to 9d a day (the artisans who executed them). The Earl of Lincoln bought an embroidered cloth for £200 – more than a lifetime's wage for a single embroiderer.

Cotton was imported from Asia and the Mediterranean, and used in its raw state for quilts and padded garments. Bokeram, a cotton cloth (the name is derived from Bokara, since it was originally imported from Asia), was used for clothes and banners. Fustian, which had a cotton weft and a linen warp, was named after Fustat in Egypt, but was also produced in Europe. Canvas was used for tents. Hemp was also employed, and linen of various qualities was used for shirts, sheets, tablecloths, towels, pillows and other items. Some cloth in Europe was block-printed with designs (though not apparently in England), and much cloth was dyed, notably in scarlet (which came from insects), blanchet (white), bluet (blue), burnet (brown), paonas (peacock blue), azure, green and murrey (mulberry), to name but a few. Marbryn was variegated, like marble, while ray was striped. Camlet was woven from angora goat hair in the Near East and elsewhere, and silk was imported both as cloth and thread. Satin originated in Zaitun in China but was also produced elsewhere. Velvet was mostly woven in Italy.

Patterned textiles became increasingly popular as time went on. Early imports had formal arrangements of animals and birds, usually in rectilinear or circular frames, but free-style designs became popular from the late thirteenth century onwards.

English centres were famous for the production of *opus Anglicanum*, embroidery in silk and gold thread. Popes delighted in English embroideries, and Matthew Paris recorded that in 1246 Pope Innocent IV ordered some from England and is engagingly credited with saying,

England is for us surely a garden of delights, truly an inexhaustible well; and from there where so many things abound, many may be extorted.

Matthew Paris added that the English merchants charged what they fancied for the material he ordered. Several popes employed an English embroiderer, Gregory of London, to work for them in the thirteenth century, while Henry III ordered embroideries from Mabel of Bury St Edmunds at various times.

Most of the surviving textiles are ecclesiastical, though the Black Prince's surcoat does survive.

Further Reading

Alexander, J. & Binski, P. (eds) *Age of Chivalry: Art in Plantaganet England 1200–1400*, London, 1987

Ashe, G. *The Quest for Arthur's Britain*, London, 1968

Ault, W. O. *Open-field Farming in Medieval England*, London, 1972

Barber, R. & Vale, J. *Tournaments: Jousts, Chivalry and Pageants in the Middle Ages*, Woodbridge, 1989

Barley, M. W. (ed.) *European Towns, Their Archaeology and Early History*, London, 1977

Barron, C. & Sutton, A. F., (eds) *Medieval London Widows, 1300–1500*, London, 1994

Beresford, M. W. *The Lost Villages of England*, London, 1954

Beresford, M. W. *New Towns of the Middle Ages*, London, 1967

Beresford, M. & Hurst, J. G. *Deserted Medieval villages: Studies*, London, 1968

Bolton, J. L. *The English Medieval Economy, 1150–1500*, London, 1985

Borg, A. *Arms and Armour in Britain*, London, 1979

Brooke, G. C. *English Coins*, London 1950

Brown, R. A. *English Castles*, London, 1976

Clarke, H. *The Archaeology of Medieval England*, London, 1984

Coppack, G. *Abbeys and Priories*, London, 1990

Cosman, M. *Fabulous Feasts: Medieval Cookery and Ceremony*, 1976

Coss, P. *The Knight in Medieval England, 1000–1400*, Stroud, 1995

Coulton, G. C. *Social Life in Britain from the Conquest to the Reformation*, Cambridge, 1918

Coulton, G. C. *Medieval Panorama*, Cambridge, 1938

Cruden, S. H. *Scottish Abbeys*, Edinburgh, 1960

Cruden, S. H. *The Scottish Castle*, Edinburgh, 1960

Cunningham, W. *Alien Immigrants to England*, (2nd edn, C. Wilson), London 1969, reprint of 1897 edn

Davis, H. W. C. *Medieval England*, London, 1928, reprint 1995

Davis, R. H. C. *The Normans and their Myth*, London, 1976

Davison, B. K. *Castles*, London, 1988

Dickinson, J. C. *Monastic Life in Medieval England*, London, 1961

Dickinson, W. C. *Scotland, from the earliest times to 1603*, London, 1961

Duncan, A. A. M. *Scotland, the Making of a Kingdom*, Edinburgh, 1975

Dunning, R. W. *Arthur: The King in the West*, Stroud, 1995

Dyer, C. *Standards of Living in the Middle Ages*, London, 1989

Eames, E. *Medieval Tiles: a Handbook*, London, 1968

Eames, P. *Furniture in England, France and the Netherlands from the Twelfth to the Fifteenth Century*, London, 1977

Evans, J. *English Art 1307–1461*, Oxford, 1949

Evans, J. A. *History of Jewellery, 1100–1870*, London, 2nd edn. 1970

Evans, J. (ed) *The Flowering of the Middle Ages*, London, 1966

Foss, M. *Chivalry*, London, 1975

Gilyard-Beer, R. *Abbeys*, London, 1959

Gimpel, J. *The Medieval Machine*, London, 1977

Goldberg, P. J. P. (ed.) *Woman is a Worthy Wight: Women in English Society, c.1200–1500*, London, 1992

Hammond, P. W. *Food and Feast in Medieval England*, Stroud, 1993

Hall, D. J. *English Mediaeval Pilgrimage*, London, 1966

Hallam, H. E. *Rural England, 1066–1348*, London, 1981

Harrison, F. L. *Music in Medieval Britain*, London, 1963

Harvey, J. *Mediaeval Gardens*, London, 1981

Hindle, B. P. *Medieval Roads*, Princes Risborough, 1982

Houston, M. G. *Medieval Costume in England and France*, London, 1939

Jones, L. E. *Old English Churches*, London, 2nd edn 1969

Keen, M. *Chivalry*, Yale, 1984

Keen, M. *English Society in the Later Middle Ages, 1348–1500*, London, 1990

King, D. J. C. *The Castle in England and Wales*, London, 1991

Laing, L. & J. *Britain's European Heritage*, Stroud, 1995

Laver, J. *A Concise History of Costume*, London, 1969

Lipson, E. *The Economic History of England, I, The Middle Ages*, London, 1947

London Museum, *Medieval Catalogue*, 1940 and reprints

Loyn, H. R. *The Norman Conquest*, London, 3rd edn 1982

Lucas, A. *Women in the Middle Ages, Religion, Marriage and Letters*, Brighton, 1983

McKinley, R. A. *A History of British Surnames*, London, 1990

McLean, T. *Medieval English Gardens*, 1981

McNeill, T. *Castles*, London, 1990

Marks, R. *Stained Glass in England during the Middle Ages*, Toronto, 1993

Mead, W. E. *The English Medieval Feast*, London, 1931, reprint 1967

Morris, R. K. *Cathedrals and Abbeys of England and Wales*, London, 1979

Myers, A. R. *England in the Late Middle Ages*, Harmondsworth, 1963

Platt, C. *The English Medieval Town*, London, 1976

Platt, C. *The Parish Churches of Medieval England*, London, 1981

Platt, C. *Medieval England, a Social History and Archaeology from the Conquest to 1600 AD*, London, 1978

Postan, M. M. *The Medieval Economy and Society*, Harmondsworth, 1976

Power, E. *The Wool Trade in English Medieval History*, Oxford, 1941

Power, E. *Medieval Women*, London, 1975

Pritchard, V. *English Medieval Graffiti*, Cambridge, 1967

Quennell, M. & C. H. B. *A History of Everyday Things in England, 1066–1499*, London, 1918

Rackham, B. *English Medieval Pottery*, London, 2nd edn 1972

Rawcliffe, C. *Medicine and Society in Later Medieval England*, Stroud, 1995

Reaney, P. H. *The Origin of English Surnames*, London, 1967

Reeves, C. *Pleasures and Pastimes in Later Medieval England*, Stroud, 1995

Rickert, M. *Painting in Britain: the Middle Ages*, Harmondsworth, 1965

Rodwell, W. *English Heritage Book of Church Archaeology*, London, 1989

Rouse, E. C. *Medieval Wall Paintings*, Princes Risborough, 1991

Rowley, T. *The Norman Heritage*, London, 1983

Rowley, T. *The High Middle Ages, 1200–1550*, London, 1986

Salzman, L. F. *English Life in the Middle Ages*, 1927

Salzman, L. F. *English Trade in the Middle Ages*, 1931

Serjeantson, M. A. *History of Foreign Words in English*, London, 1935

Steane, J. M. *The Archaeology of Medieval England and Wales*, London, 1985

Stenton, D. M. *English Society in the Early Middle Ages, (1066–1307)*, Harmondsworth, 1952

Stewart, I. *The Scottish Coinage*, London, 2nd ed. 1967

Stone, L. *Sculpture in Britain: the Middle Ages*, Harmondsworth, 1955

Taylor, C. C. *Village and Farmstead*, London, 1983

Taylor, C. C. *The Archaeology of Gardens*, Aylesbury, 1983

Thomas, M. W. (ed.) *A Survey of English Economic History*, London, 1957

Turner, H. L. *Town Defences in England and Wales, 900–1500*, London, 1971

Mitchell, W. R. *The Haunts of Robin Hood*, Clapham, 1970

Wagner, A. R. *Heralds and Heraldry in the Middle Ages*, Oxford, 2nd edn 1956

Webb, G. *Architecture in Britain: the Middle Ages*, Harmondsworth, 1956

Williams, M. & Echols, A. *Between Pit and Pendulum, Women in the Middle Ages*, Princeton, 1994

Yeomans, P. *Medieval Scotland*, London, 1996

Index